WHERE THE RIVER KEEPS NO GODS

With Extended Selections

Cliff M. Richeal

ISBN: 978-0-578-19556-8 (sc)
ISBN: 978-1-4834-7917-0 (e)

Library of Congress Control Number: 2018900266

rev. date: 02/19/2018

This book is for friendship (Steve, John, Joe, Todd),
love of language, family, and other such fascinations
that keep one alive and curious to the end.

"But I tried, didn't I? Goddammit, at least I did that."
—R. P. McMurphy, *One Flew Over the Cuckoo's Nest*

Contents

At the Top

Vertical and with a
pulse, the obligatory
day begins.

Your clothes don't fit.
Your hours won't keep.

The chain of life begins
to slip on you
of this sprocket-tooth world—
its Ferris-wheel symmetry—
keeps heart tricking your
eyes along a linear logic.

You get fired. Your
tears won't take the ride.
Your mind locks.

You consider it: Am I
stuck at the top of my life,
with all gears stripped,
all teeth lost,
and with no possibility
that it's just a dream
from which I'll wake
and simply come down?

Sleeps

A man wakes up. In the end, he'll know very little
about his relationship to the universe. He will never
say that he conversed successfully with a tree. He
won't have coffee on a Saturday with a walnut that
asks him to please pass the sugar, the cream, and so on.

A man wakes up. In the beginning, he'll set out with
boyhood charm, a naive beauty, and with the understanding
that honesty is best policy or that love isn't a trick, and so on.

During his start and finish, a man will slowly learn how
to go deeper and deeper into his sleep. His dreams will begin
to falsify certain claims. His heart will be subject to the rules
used in boyhood celebrations—that's
    right, the dangling piñata.
And his hot coffee will begin to meet his lips forever cold.

But still, a man wakes up. He rises, not knowing why
exactly. Where his best coordinates are hiding, ah,
he could not say. But he walks and remembers occasionally
a time when love filled out his chest and removed
the poisoned darts from his stopgap heart. He even runs,
meandering with his start-to-stutter stops like a chased
duck, hoping with a sense of earned fear that triple-stepping
his waddle will bring closer his needle-
    black eyes to the water
where he'll glide godlike and release his soul onto the air,
and alas, bend ever forward slowly into
    the deepest of his sleeps.

The First Hour of Fall

Begin as if those first-lost leaves rushing over
the road's tired coda of Goodyear and makeshift
repair have nothing to do with how this scene
brings your heart toward an optimum transience.

The oncoming flurry and flush from lost petals—
now aching from holding up their end of the bargain,
content to let go of stem and root, of spring's opening,
as well as summer's cutting off—sunlight and water.

To love the world from other spaces
and reassemble as a foreign discord of eventual
acceptance—this is the only way beauty will have us.

My lovers, the trees, all losing strength for me—
the tipped apple cart or red wheelbarrow—abandoning
the stressful patterns of day and in place of it all
the image world unlocked by nature's cyclic call.

Just follow the shady trail, running as wild and with
such brutal intent, as if to think some animal
will be tracked and taken, the caught kill now silent.
And here the first-lost leaves rush overtly over it all.

I hear it now: the first hour of fall.

When the Poet Cannot Speak

The doctor said he all but lost his hearing,
but others say he hears when
he needs and otherwise
he don't need to hear a thing.

When he did speak,
the language tried to untie
the severe knots of human failure
or the noose that kept circling
to knot his deaf-and-dumb heart.

There's always a woman
in the ending; the beginning
too—less conspicuous, though,
not that clear shot at the ending.

But then it takes direct aim
with an intent to finalize
the kill.

Who fired it? They may never say.

Who felt it? Neither
collects the blame.
He's deaf now, so let him be.

Talking is for the hearing,
but after this,
he don't seem to hear a thing.
Talking is for the hearing; are
you listening to him at all?

When It Sleeps

It does not hurt when it sleeps.
A far distance presides over
its living seizures so that a
welcome calm pulls

thorns and acreage of pains
and gone-wrong fellowship
from its tender-moving flesh—

red.

It does not hurt when it sleeps,
the nights filled with faint
spaces of preexistence,
inside and united,
safely drawn before humanity.

This red mushroom bursting
from within us, working out its
own life from downbeat number one,
until its coffin-closed whole-note resting,

whereupon it does not hurt, and I, its
holder, can go the way of
the human heart.

Sleep, adrift, passing through my
existence before it's ever
taken shape.

What Little Has Been Done

for Steve and Kelly

Here the frost is implacable.
From the north, the lowering
episodes of an unknown winter wait
like a hungry skulk, circling
through Arctic winds, moving into
the absolute white bite of winter's
elongated maw.

Neighbors begin their final descent
across the way, forging their final
lawn cut, leaf pickup, or the insertion
of yet another layer of distance between
the world and people who try to live in it.

The dawn of spring hope all but gone,
the summer liquor cabinet locked.

Inside the crunch of piled-up leftover leaves
is where the thinking begins, the unsettling trap
of heart, because humans now, here, must
answer those open-ended questions that
have been sitting on the front porch for months,
or stowed away in the garage, or left as plain absent.

Here the loss is irreversible.
From the south, the rising
patterns of a foreseeable future leave
like a skein of untagged geese, outward

into the memory of minds, each
equivocal yet determined
about what little has been done.

Our lives, our loves,
still so much to do.

Those Goddamn Daffodils

Those goddamn daffodils report back to me
each and every spring, telling and retelling
the story of how I continue to repeat my life.

From this office window, I hear their gossip.
They spy on me during meetings and
while I'm on the phone. They take in the
rain and respond to the world in a most
natural way, a growth through dependency.

Here on this desk: financial statements,
network topographies, a dense senility
of system analysis and data-driven results.
I manage the characters on the paper
as if each were a hopeful fragment of my life.

The daffodils continue in their ardent bloom
to ask that I convert this lifeless life of
mine into a more purposeful refrain,
one not so unlike their own, one in which
the present is predicated upon the past
and the future continues to release itself
in a more pure and relatable fashion.

To say nothing ever changes is to admit
to oneself that the author of one's own
life has done little to pour out new and
inviting chapters or to move forward
the dull plot, in its place a dead ovary,
a lapsing scene in which the film

clips and claps on a coda-driven
synapse of failure and repeat, a drone.

I repeat my sad renewal as if it were
a contract to self, the circular argument
playing as a vintage album whose
needle keeps sipping from its coffee
until its tongue, wagging north to south wildly,
lips the dull china,
reminds me I alone must resurrect myself.

The Elusive Catching of Time

Try to catch time or seal space between
the indefinite conclusions of your life.

Once a boy, hand held under rushing river,
pouring its gush out, relieving the rock-side
pressure, the force of too much intimacy.

Try to kiss the air and pretend its response
has any feeling at all; it's all just a hung lull.

As a man, truth dies beneath the exaggeration
of humankind—what it does to climb the ladder
of American misery, with its pleading
passivity pawned off as actionable wedding
vows, or its smile-you're-on-the-boss's-clock
kind of acting, slicing up of colleagues while
posturing on about integrity, etiquette, or
why it's important not to openly kill a man.

Mostly it all gets lost to a great piece of ass
on a Saturday night, one that goes well with the
curtains but cannot say how or when it arrived.
The inevitable and impossible are always happening.

So try to catch time or seal space between
the indefinite conclusions of your life.
The vast heart will escape you—as a boy and
as a man, always seeking the
elusive catching of time. Seek on, my strangers.

On Any Afternoon

Where the rose does not bloom or the
    heart widen any afternoon,
you'll find a life chance anew—the truest
    moment in a series of falsities.

It is much too easy, you see, to kneel and
    settle alongside the dead.
The challenge in living is to rise steadily
    and walk in a world of life.

Get to the symmetry. Allow this geometry, its
    lines and points, its exceptional
intersections, to unravel and necessarily connect
    that which needs to be attached.

The ligaments and bones have no opinion
    on the matter. Oh, but the soul, it
is the preacher and pulpit, the apolitical
    proposition of our very existence.

Collect its voice—this butterfly of all
    reason—and then let it sing until
your life fills with a kind of hearing, a full
    encounter with a complete melody
where the rose must always bloom and the
    heart widens on any afternoon.

Vaporize

I consider it
nights when lonely begins to take on new dimensions,
if and when I can no more sleep than I can find cause to live

in this overly cerebral state where starlight obsesses,
takes hold of its white canvas until no night appears at all.

I climb into the back closet of my mind. I do the math.
Numbers are a severe sense of hope: that money might
come of it, that two ringlets of ceremony can control much,
or that the mileage our very bodies take
        on is in fact an odometer.

In here, I survey the audio of a grandfather clock, ticktocking
on my rocking heart, its warped bony phrases of body,
so suspenseful, a spring cocks and mallet
        dongs, leaving me and others
with one less second on our minds, but
        also, with more reason
to let go of timing itself: a fermata that cannot, will not end in
this universe of ideas—the cosmic palette
        of play, of playing its song.

The basement steps creek like an old
        water pump—but only when
the ghosts of burden makeshift their bodies into voodoo
mannequins of form and discontent, the
        ripe kind that comes to get you.

Get down from there, they say; come here and enjoy your life.
I am beyond their curtain. The play has
    emboldened the audience
within me such that I quiver and lose track of the many parts
of this composition. There was a first note, I am certain of it.

Can you just stay down there? I say. Or
    must it begin, troublesome,
and with low tones of cello rising narrowly
    through the chimney's
vertical corridor, here where, if I remove my eyes and detach
my ears, the fears of consideration will
    upwardly slowly vaporize?

Here a constant minute, whose unsettling overtures reach up
through the throat of the hollowed house to grip what's left
of me and to settle some score I must
    have somehow unsettled.

Tremors

These varied tremors of our evolution
shift like missed feelings in the night.

For all of the earth's lithosphere and study,
still, some things won't ever budge.

Our hearts,
deep and dark and delicate—
the way our hopes hold that a kiss should keep.

We kneel and cry at the center of our
troubling universe, reverse, and
beg no questions any longer; instead,
simply split, as in an atom, and swim
into the nearest embryo of each new day.

These tremors et al.
It's okay not to know.

Time

The truth about time is that it has no owner.
Our lives play out in time,
though nearly everything is still
to be announced: the graduation,
the marriage, the employment opportunity,
the accident on the ice, or the unexpected death.

And yet, time is showing us everything
all the while. If we dare scan the life-scape
and click-picture the development of it all,
it all is readily available at will.

We seek out an owner,
as if it owes us something
of a favor or a rainbow-colored
lollipop.

Time rages like no river we've ever known,
running the wild rainwater
of our lives through the earth's veins,
into red clay and old Indian drum circles,
until the roar and splash of unknowingness
settles into a bellowing echo,
where peace and sunlight idle,
and for a moment,
you hear your announcement

playing out in time, as if life has somehow
timed this all perfectly.

The Unjust World for Idiots

And if you believe all men are created equal,
then you may be our best candidate for idiot-elect.

Above all, the adjective rules; no other part of
speech so accurately installs or disposes of men.

Short. Bald. Ruthless. Clever. Whatever you
choose just underscore it all with a certain
notion of bias. Oh, you say a bad word: bias.

Discrimination—say it isn't so. You bastard!

You aim to say the world is not on nature's
terms: ideal, leveled, fair, just, simple or true?
How dare you?

I just heard a tree fall. It did. Just fall
down again.
What will you do about it?

The Relentless Pursuit of Evermore

The years have forged me,
worn me down to the skeleton's frame.
I've handcuffed cynicism to the bedpost
and warned all newcomers:
There is no key; get out before the pain sets in.

The patterns and sexual derivatives are
not sustainable, no matter how honestly
your parents and friends carry out their own lies.

Life is natural and therefore always ending
the mere palatable pleasures that we
curate on our own terms. And all the while,
a foggy trust is the best we ever know
becomes the untouchable ether.

You can only hold a lover in your arms
for so long before
a cryptic distance claims itself,
gives birth to farther distances, until an expanse
reveals a truth about your uninterrupted
emptiness.

You reach to fetch your feelings,
but the adjudication is over as
a warm glow from a cold star
leaves you and your lover
breathlessly out of time and
out of sync.

Off in the furthest distance of
your mind, you hear two stars
collide, and pieces explode
into sub-structural nodes of nothing.
It is happening again:

We are back online, moving
inexorably toward the relentless
pursuit of evermore.

The Boy and the Rat

The boy cloonked with his baseball spikes
into the dusty heart
of their musty, boned basement space.

A rat who'd taken
to calling the east ledge his own
stared like a mad crow
while the boy crumbled
into a hill of dirty laundry.

His tears taken in by holed
sports socks, him holding them,
feeling the spirit of some dogged
immigrant work through him,
leave him a history, a blueprint
for pain, misjudgment, and destiny.

The world may have begun this way.
He considered it.
Man seeking asylum from himself,
troubled sunlight encouraging weeds.

When the mother calls out to him,
there is no longer a boy that hears.
The rat scurries down and alongside
the boy—a warning of some kind.
Again, the mother places a firm
request for response, but the boy,
having now gone deaf inside of his
own blank world, decides decisions

are more than a choice, that keeping
safe is about hiding the very distance
between all people, places, and things.

After the light is turned on him,
white absence clears the room of everything.
The rat goes blind, curls up into
the crumble of the fallen boy,
and what happens next won't ever heal a thing.

The Good Life

To sing and weep and remember that once
    you were a boy who could
not dream of becoming a man:

That was the good life!

Thatch

It takes years of derelict neglect.
Thousands of days will pass before
you find nothing has been growing.
No water or light has touched or
caressed this abandoned soil.
Too dark and forgotten is it,
the outside world has lost
all interplay with its nine
distinct and interlocking parts.
In a word, the grass plants
are decomposing furiously,
reaching peak and claiming
death as a last and final resort.

Alarm!

Questions about your own life
begin to sprout—weeds that
eventually intertwine with florets,
which in turn group into spikelets,
and finally a family form: inflorescences.
Sounds romantic, right?
Sounds like something's at play.

But you yourself have given up the idea,
men and women capable
of pure light and water,
the nutrients-inherent,
the ones we need for love's sake.

You take up with the rake.
One Ames True Temper
reaches the scene.
Fifteen and a half inches
of pure, heavy-duty thatching rake;
multi-purpose:
cultivates soil and dethatches your lawn;
and with a fifty-four-inch handle. Damn!

Within the first cycle of reaching out
and gliding back the rake to your chest,
your ambivalence checks itself.
In its place, a certain concern, if not fully
blown epiphany: an entire world of
species and subspecies are collected.
Could this be your Galapagos Islands?
And if so, what might Darwin have said
about the dead, the living,
the exposed nomenclature of our desires?
I know—sounds romantic, right?
Sounds like something's definitely at play.

You call her back after fifteen months
of absence, not quite thinking much of
anything more. You are drunk and tired,
and the thatching thing has got you down.
A digitally recorded diatribe explains
her inability or unwillingness to "come to
the phone." There are many reasons why,
not so unlike the forgotten soil
and the newly expired grass plants.
Sometimes, you just have to thatch.
It isn't romantic, and it doesn't take into
account the deliberate neglect you've

placed upon the pressure points in
yours and other people's lives.
Basically, you're just pulling a fucking
rake to and fro, hoping the net collection
can be easily bagged and put out to curb,
forgotten, or at best,
passed on for the worry and troubles of others.

Anyone but you.

Shooting Grubs

These northeast birds, with all of their terrific varietals,
begin sing-song and chatter as early as 4:43 a.m.
It's May. The world hasn't changed, only the earth
has turned on its axis, turning on nature; the egg-timer!
The birds have to be singing about something, don't they?

As one who has never slept well, and especially
with a lover loafed upon his chest, I fall from previous
evening into the lightest of sleep, turning my thoughts
ahead, as if there is some human saving time
that will allow for these sounds to prematurely reach me.

Yesterday and around five-ish, I began work in the front yard,
removing grub-sucked grass, which had been,
as a result, converted into yards of plaintiff thatch.

With each scorch-tear and loose-knit snap of grass,
they were exposed—these white C-shaped grubs,
the larval stage of beetles, revealed for every neighbor to see.

If I was a cowboy, I might have pulled off my hat and
dust-thawped it against my thigh: *Dangummit*!

But it's year the 2010. I used a more current vernacular:
Goddammit, son-of-a-bitch, you little motherfuckers!

They just squirmed there, like an insidious group of
helpless embryos: We didn't do nothing … not us,
you got the wrong grubs, mister.

The birds.

Without delay, I ripped up twelve hundred square feet
of grub-sucked grass, as if I was revealing to the world itself:
Look here, my yard's been wearing a toupee—
ta-da!

It's 4:45 a.m. as I capture the conclusion with my
Sony Cyber-Shot. The birds, all varietals, sweep in
and onto the scene. It's a spring breakfast, about which
they'll be happily sing-songing for springs to come.

As for the grubs, I assume they will peddle back
into some life-cycle, as their god sees fit.
For now, I am camera-clicking the death of each
of them, and with each click, whistling a
tune that echoes from each morning hereafter.
Loosely translated: Die, motherfuckers, die;
die, motherfuckers;
and so on …

Simpleminded Fairy Gods of Government

Democracy is two wolves and a lamb
voting on what to have for lunch.
Liberty is a well-armed lamb contesting the vote!
—Benjamin Franklin

There is this taut sense that I will soon snap,
    paint the house in spring, and be gone
from it all by fall. You see, recently I learned

the bank note is a fraud. Who knows, but some
    old Indian god, where loan and
ownership begin and end. Fabled policy:

eminent domain, compulsory purchase,
    resumption, or expropriation; they all
steal using fabricated linguistic measures; hoping to high

hell, the common man will understand
    this kind of ownership.

Those tax-and-spend liberal rabbit hearts,
    those kill-em-all right-wingers.
All acting in complicity to hate, hurt, and
    demote the American purpose.

I stand without dignity; I crawl without job. And I ask you—
you who have stolen and sold our body
    parts to foreigners: When
can an American be one again?

What new war must we the people learn
    about in our history-future
in order to reclaim a day of decency, a
    month of normalcy, or a year
we might once again call our own?

This here is no freedom. I am not free with
    my tongue. It has been tied
by bureaucracy and those too afraid to hear
    the very words once defended,
no matter their frivolity or significance. For
    it once was all a welcome say.

Today, I scream out to you: Hiroshima!
    I further the call: Nagasaki!

You did it to them, and you'll do it to us: We
    the people, made like them,
of a sensitive skin that tears and burns
    under such doomed acts,
which clunks a thousand skulls high when
    dropped into dumpsters.

You misdiagnose those signatures: Jefferson,
    Franklin, and Adams. And
soon, I fear, you will misdiagnose the
    urgency and desire of a man and
woman to steer clear of fools and simpleminded
    fairy gods of government.

The charge will be treason, and for no other
    reason, than to annihilate and
distance themselves from any semblance of
    all that you have willingly wronged.

Their spirit, their will. These things
    American you shall never have,
dear sir and madam. We shall take you to
    the tar and then to the feather,
until humility finds you, or until a new
    revolution sends you all back to the
hell from where you came ...

Second Tuesday of Next Week

Your Monday turns Thursday turns
Sunday back into a Tuesday
as Wednesday feels like a Saturday
and Friday just won't fit your needs.

These are days. Days define us
properly and otherwise. Decide.

Monday this, Friday that,
Saturday just sat, and Sunday
went more like a Tuesday or Wednesday
save for that second when Thursday
put you on like a new pair of jeans.

These are days. Days remind us
figuratively and otherwise. You sigh.
Why?

My love left Wednesday, hers last
Friday, ours two Saturdays ago, before
Tuesday was a Monday and Thursday
turned Sunday. She turned on me,
When will you love me, when?

I do say, my love,
the second, second Tuesday of next week.
Look here, it's right here on the schedule,
Tuesday it is.

Picnic Spirit

You'll one day swim toward a shore that researchers
have systematically removed—during some
testing phase—maybe when they sought to
virtualize the existence of some animal or being.
You'll cry, not so unlike a beaten and eaten
roadside crow, now flat and vulnerable.

Then, just when hope hears your last confession,
you most likely will sprout a fever and command
things of your indelible and frequented past.

A harshly staged production of your life.
Begin with a monologue—your mother in print dress,
so young, free, able-bodied, and denying
your father no love whatsoever. He enters
stage left and for thirteen years stares at his
wife. The audience disapproves, suggests we
get him off stage, but not before he leaves you
with welts and darkly constructed criticism.

During intermission, you notice you've gone gray.
They are out of wine. People begin to spring
for the doors, agreeing that your life is a one-act play.

What's happened to you? You've lost all of
your picnic spirit. What's more, I've packed
us fresh ham salad. What kind of a life will
we have if we can't sit simply and eat
all of this happily? I'd like to think there's

more, to you, for us, than stale bread and half-eaten arguments, which I always find are our best leftovers—when the curtains fall, and the audience in your mind goes frightfully silent.

Permanency

A death gets no more permanent.

From the arrow to the nuclear skyline, our achievements
dwindle by comparison—

the absolute commitment to killing off potential outright.

Hear the trumpeter holding his note during the silenced
night, the subtracted hemisphere of his ghostly heart.

He pressures the left-handed ghost, the interrogation never
fulfilled, always backtracking over a fact—missed or let go.

The summer rocks potato-sacked and swung into a violent
protest, just wanting for a certain relevant fact to show itself.

The spring showing, the natural art gallery—a fainting
come back to life—or whatever presence we'll assign it.

The fall overture abandons the last uptight citizen. This,
a cold remembering, failed survival,
        the instants between why
and however explode; and the rushed
        judgment collected in butterfly
fashion, kept beyond its own intentions,
        until a next attempt arrives.

The winter as prodigal son, as William Cullen Bryant or a
fast-shadow recall of Jean-Francois Champollion; but these,
these are not the days of his life, not now—not when winter
translates its own hieroglyphics or now-forgotten poetic lines.

Out, into a razor-thin cut of red heart burning, erasing really,
using nature to steal nature, or just allowing
    it to safely assume its end.

And if a death gets no more permanent (than this), then okay.
Close your doors, knuckle down your
    windows, and turn your seasons
like a deadbolt, knowing how few things
    can return easily to the
open position: a heart, a coffin, or a crevice
    without the correct key.

Our Sometimes-Empty Shells

Sun stroked over the ice-cold homes,
as I stood barely naked in the driveway,
drunk and collapsible—a fume to the
earth,
and wondering on and on about my
middle-life. I am here, and what will
I make of it?

The songs, crazy and dancing in my
skull,
lonely and quivering among these
just natural elements.

How does a man fail so well
and so often?

I cannot control this breeze that fills me,
and with it, takes down the snowflake
to the ground. It's where I am:

Ever-embarrassed, dead upon
the find.

Metronome

I am of the opinion that metronome marks go for nothing. As far
as I know,
all composers have, as I, retracted their
metronome marks in later years.
—Johannes Brahms

From Galileo to the forefathers of the finest
    composition, we have decided
the metronome is either a valuable and
    instructive device, or that it
is of little use, if only because what becomes
    mechanized is no longer human.

But the human does mark time, and by
    no choosing of his own.

Each increment, in between his very
    heartbeat, equal. The hundreds
of thousands of incalculable synapses burst and click, kicking
off into a steady circuitry, working to
    keep our various levels of life
online and prudently intertwined as an
    emotional, vital, stronghold.

Or is ours really a case of tempo rubato, the human
encasement, the flesh, its loose wiring and spastic firings-off
of memory—retrieval and archival, of its
    permanent flux and *felt* sense of time
during our animal-instinct scenarios of
    sport, sexual pleasure, and of
fighting for, where appropriate, our very survival?

To clock our existence would be to limit our very humanness.
For music, even more so—to lock down the beats and reduce
their own lives to within each and every
        measured millisecond.

If it must be used, then save it for the
        marching, the troops, for
those bellicose encounters that require
        we marry our machinery
to our humanness under the extenuating circumstances
in which we must regard our ill-measured
        movements as justified.

Large-Breasted Ballerina

I'd say love has about the same odds:

a large-breasted ballerina
gracefully top-spinning into
the exactitude of physics
and bodily nuance

while toting the full bounty
of nature's stereotypical feed.

What is it that you want from me?

That nature can be altered for the
good of man is simply not a plan,
my dear. I am the large-breasted
ballerina—hopeful, but bound by
laws that cannot at will be changed.

I Know, I Knew, I Say These Things Are True

Weighing in on the seconds against the years you know,
you knew.

Happiness is alarming,
and so when it happens—as infrequently as it does—
there's a sense, not in our taking stock of it.
That part comes much later as it packs
    its things and leaves your life,
rarely as it found it. But rather, it remembers you
as a few seconds considered within all the years
we know, we knew.

Time is a terrifying bedfellow. Its constant turning and
chirping, reminding us that the day is not comprised of
seconds, minutes, hours, and evenly as years,
at least, not as our minor league school teachers would have
had us believe. Time is in itself an unknowable universe.
(Mistakenly we relate its comings and goings to our life.)

Feelings are the fleas that fester as wildfire within our hearts.
What else to say about those things?

Weighing in on the seconds against the years you know,
you knew.

It would become harder, more difficult
    with each passing minute,
to understand how the hour passes, or where exactly
a week has gone. The math tends to get sketchy, as your

heart slowly slows
down
into everything you now swear you know, you knew,
yet cannot prove because the heart itself becomes, as I
say, sketchy.

Weighing in on the seconds against the years you know,
you knew, but for the life of you cannot or will not prove.

How Darkness Awakes Within Us

Darkness calls
within us all, heritable variations
passed down
through centuries of unstoppable
assimilation.

Call it the politics of genetics,
or put more simply: inhumane nature,
played out, such as it is, within us.

God-cards splayed, counted—ah,
the exactitude of it all.

Then the face cards of anger, jealousy,
spite, reverse diplomacy; yes, the death cards
keep coming until the final hand is lost.

Now, then, your lover goes, your job
is exposed, and you collapse under
the weight of some unkind deceptive
immoral geometry in which space
no longer gets measured.

Darkness relieves you of tools,
of mathematics, of any such
higher effort or reasoning.

You sit among the endless
moons, endless skies of trying to think,
but you can no longer think;
therefore, you aren't.

Happenstance

I

As it turns out, the life you planned
is one that had not planned on you.
So true, the roses did go about their spiral way,
last June.

But by the age of thirty-seven, you had developed
what would later be called a cocktail heart.
No love without gin or bourbon,
certainly no purpose without drunken miscues or
dropped silverware.

Every spring you spoke of starting over—
using clichés and metaphors
to make the announcement.

Then the news: the girl of your dreams died,
first kiss, late-to-prom, all of it, used memories,
leaving nothing, no leftovers
of entitlement or human deed, no luck.

When your mother came to visit,
her references to your limited success—
career, relationships, etc.,
split the last hair between you: no hug goodbye.

Your neighbors worry that maybe time
has made too much or not enough of you.
At this point, you are old, they
have bills to pay, and winter is closing in.

II

I heard them first, and then watched
the red sirens scream up the street.
The underpaid ambulance workers
answering the last call of the night.

The paper paraphrased your death
in no more than a paragraph—leaves
behind, was an X, Y, or Z, attended
church—the usual, really. The usual.

I wonder, in the middle of it all,
Have they, in their own weary state,
passed me by, hurried wrongly,
relied somehow on
bad information?

They don't hear me, do they?

And so help is not on the way.

Flower Cluster

This paniculate
and delicate
life of yours
and mine:

A so-easily sailable
lip-push of feather dust,
in the face of some
unknown absolute.

Cancer, crash,
strapped-for-cash,
or any other inalterable loss
that crosses our paths.

Indeterminate, this flowered
cluster—the human life.

Breathe where you are able,
sing when you can,
and draw sunlight and water
into your veins,
as if the remainder will always
carry.

Try not to distance
yourself too far—
temporal being no less
than forever, just a
matter of mathematics,
which we'll not concern
ourselves with here.

File Restore

The common maze of days, in and out,
until your source file is lost.

Every area scans itself
for some traceable algorithm.

An old hymn hums from behind an old
sofa bed, where as a child, you took
yourself, then let yourself go.

Remember me? Who are you now?
We're the same, are we not?
Get out!

The key you kept
under it all, as years began to lock you up,
forget they knew you.

A combination: pure fear mixed
with a deadly shame. You alien.

But inside the maze of days, memory
clicks like old high school drumsticks
counting toward something, or away,

to inherit and adopt the fragile comfort
of mental affliction—a skewed
version of yourself walking about
inside a locked body of circuitry.

Click, hit, double-click, swipe,
turn, click, swipe, hit, hit, click.
Your turn; you do: file restored.

Eye-Latching

I eye-latch onto the western sky to find
    a narrow-hoped hallway,
inside of which a world of cosmic nouns
bounces and rebounds repeatedly, until sanity loses
all of its remains, the way luggage goes missing,
or the way you wake years later to kiss your lover's lips,
even though no lover now feels your revolving efforts.

There is at the caustic center a terrible pull of human
anecdote when the western sky repeats itself and
the record of your life is liable to play endlessly

throughout the bare-star galaxy of missed transmissions
and overtly trip-hop moons, each tagged and studied, as if
knowledge and passion are somehow
    conceivably compatible.

And as these night crickets tweet and the lightning bugs
sleep tightly about their own worlds,
I eye-latch onto a small space of happiness,
    a memory never again
surpassed by late nights of well-intentioned goal-setting
or the ignition of a promising career that in the end fails.

I eye-latch onto a black night filled by hundreds of
thousands of contiguous white bubbles—soap-spawned
orbits of silent clarity floating randomly and with no
fear at all that I or the atmosphere could at any time
pop their molecules, dismiss their existence, or in
any way interrupt them within the fullest
    contest of their being.

Driftwood

Sitting like a piece of driftwood on the embankment
of someone's lost eternity,

and with only a sense of squatter's rights
ruminating between the lines of adverse possession
and all that has in my dented life been taken from me.

The mirror's instincts to reflect, the soul's boastful
mirage that shimmers over my heart as if its quivering
red river idles in a state of absolute and permanent redress.

After dinner and pints of stout
have been wildly transient
throughout my
body and bloodstream—
the wire-flesh veins and arterial lenses—
I see through all of it, a hoping and hoaxing
by the self, how it will finally grasp
the one failed belief about its life.

Man is built to expire. No warranties or attorney fees.
No prayers to any god or gospel will
salvage the bones or resell its finest hours back
for hock or otherwise.
It's the temporal and beautiful that fill in life,
as it portends itself some sense of ownership and capsule,
of self-delegated sovereignty.

The lonely part is coming. Acres and acres of it.
Has been here for some. Will find the others,
sitting like driftwood with only a sense of squatter's rights
ruminating between the lines of adverse possession
and all that with time will take from us our very lives.

Breaking Spines

You break your fear as you would
snap the spine of a waiting twig.

Grab and grip sorrow as you might
ring the sulking red cloth
that holds the blood of your dying mother.

Reach over and hold your brother
as you might cradle
your very first dream.

Kiss the air,
where gone missing are your loves,
their curves, never-ending,
their smiles, and the pain you've provided them with—
a rich and deep everlasting sea.

Charter this expanse, as you allow yourself
[air]
rising from the bottom floor, in blue and orange,
your flames singing and crackling as
a piled sink-ship of a thousand burning twigs:

hear their spines all breaking an ocean's worth
of fear.

Blue Summer

The first day of a blue summer—
long, is about to click
in the blink

of our cog-knowledged hearts.

The free whirly chirp of some
sparrow,
gone desperate into a pebble-skipped flight
through a not-so-sovereign sky,
where mechanization survives
for a time,
this blue summer; the sun will not die.

The first day of a blue summer—
song is about to sing,
in the blink

of our sprocket-springed lives.

Here the dull differential between a
failed math and a moral uprising
carries the burden of both our
work and worry; but the sun will not die.

The first day of a blue summer—
delayed, is about to stall,
before the fixed

recycled minds of an increasingly inattentive America.

These halls of knowledge and justice
where man powers over man as if
we might lobotomize our lands as well
as its caretakers into a calm and accepting
space of sequestered passivity; but the sun will not die.

Inside of our boardrooms and cubicles,
where people stake their lives, uproot their
better judgment, and provide actionable deliverables,
because sustenance dictates their failing chain
of survivalist theory; and still, the sun will not die.

The first day of a blue summer—
the sun, not now nor ever,
will die before man.
This, the first day of a blue summer,
is where the sparrow follows inward
toward his home,
singing deeply within himself
along due-course winds:
inform his flight, direct his path's
delight on this
first day of a blue summer,
where before all is said and done, the sun will not die,
and the sparrow will listen evermore to his heart.

Frail Nature

The frail nature of human atrophy slips unevenly
through our lives, like a set of overly used gears,
teeth chipped and size now inconsequential—
the lowest gear no longer a part of a formal hierarchy—
as our intended differential steadily expands.

Our people eyes shakily spy,
though our receptors offer little more than
dirty lenses and misinformation.
Who can make out any of this?

These aging fields of blank harvest
pitted against the surreal memory
of a rainbow canvas called childhood.
It's the distance that's getting to me.

If we were among some indigenous tribe,
you could (without consequence) slice
my skin, no different than an American
following the penetrated flesh-cut of a fish,
and you might fish out a rib or two,
go free-form insane, and break out into tongues,
while I stare remotely into
the stayed reflection of a brought mirror,
my skin, its loss, or my people eyes
crying with no formal remedy.

You might dance drunkenly around a fire
until that bone takes to ash,
and you might settle alongside of
what is left of me, to makeshift in your mind
that we're okay, that life doesn't end this way.

I will, of course, have since slipped,
like an overly used gear, no longer
able to catch or catch up or otherwise
find my proverbial footing.
I will have moved beyond the full
measure of my very specific and
intended death,

a frail nature in utero-atmospheric motion,
hedging a bet on the next life,
maybe even subliminally hopeful.
it happens. Maybe.

You Come to the Poem

for Amy

Act I: You Come to the Poem

You come to the poem when the world
    will no longer come to you.

It happens as an old love arrives in town.
    It's noon, but it's also late fall,
and the sun's prescription of sunlight is about to near its end.

You follow her shadow onto the Interstate, where the
miscellaneous traffic warns you, and where you
feel the engine's pulse begin to slow. It is late fall.
Soon, spring will separate all of this from the winter.

You say to yourself what you know you
    can no longer say to her.
She has placed a kind hand on the situation. But upon that
hand, a ringlet of commitment, one that
    informs your heart that
lives are at stake here, that their love will not take a back seat
to your newborn knowledge. The heart requires a maturity;
the heart desires a certain sincerity. Now and only now, you
feel prepared with a full understanding, and you think you
might follow that shadow home, knock on its owner's door,
and forget for a brief moment about how girls like her are
the ones with whom you make a life that holds a sky of love
and an immeasurable world of complete faith and happiness.

You want all of this and more. But it's fall, sundown, and so
you come to the poem when the world
    will no longer come to you.

Act II: The Knock

Knock, knock, knock.

Hi. I'm here. It's me. Remember? Look, I have changed. It's—
well—it's okay now. Really, I'm different in so many ways.
It's really quite amazing, and I have come
    to share all of this with you.
Remember? We were in love. You told me so many times.
You said, "Now here's a man I could love for all the
right reasons." You said it just like that. How good of me to
recall your words, as if it hasn't in fact been seven years.
All of it, right here, right now. I mean,
    nothing's really changed
between us. Sure, a little time. Time will happen with or
without us, but look at us; we're still young. It's okay.
I am so glad I am here to share all of this with you today.

Act III: Back to Planet Earth

Dear poem, I fear there isn't enough of you to cover the
heart-tender breakage this time. You always know just
what to say and how exactly to put it directly enough.

She's gone. The Interstate is a city of ghost-cars,
sifting winter and breathing old exhaust fumes,
so that love is nowhere in this sky to be found.
I am lonely and suddenly unable to discern
age from happiness, knowledge from triumph.
It's as if the only known pulse is a girl, whose

skin I will never again know, whose lips are
lost behind the curtains of an abandoned play,
and whose heart was once my gentle monologue-
turned-unreliable dissertation. My every whole fear
is happening here in real time. It's still fall, sundown, so
I come to you because the world will no longer come to me.

Utah

for Kristine

The way the sun went down that day
should have led me to the facts:
You, too, were leaving me,

and in ways that were also only
visual: your slow and unresponsive
kisses, which never really reached me;
the structural flaws in our lovemaking;
or those breeding, monosyllabic answers
lovers recite mostly at the end of it all.

But there was three thousand miles to cover.
California wanted you back, and quickly Ohio
by contrast became the dismal d-mark of
a failed—not withstanding a few minor
successes—trial, love's complete withdrawal.

Gone from your imagination was my chiseled body
and wholesome Midwest character, each now replaced
with mediocrity and just-some-guy, whose high
opinion of himself led him toward more lies
than truth-telling, though it was the lies (he argued)
that bought for each a few more hours of smiling.

We reached Lincoln, Nebraska, at 1:00 a.m., having
driven for nearly twelve hours without hesitation.
The only vacancy was host to shag carpet, bedbugs,
and walls, whose nicotine addiction was at least
forty years in the making. Here was a metaphor-appropriate
anecdote for how badly things had gone.

Somewhere during the next forty-eight hours
we watched trains heading back east pass us
as I privately thought of your father—his love of trains
and how their own existence is a kind of teeter-totter,
linear process, picking up people and things,
but then, also, the pure utility of it all:
the eventual dropping off of everything in life.

Over a McDonald's Egg McMuffin in Utah, I placed my plastic
orange cup firmly down and got serious for a minute. I was
about to break, and to express with
    real tears, how sorry I was,
that not one goddamned thing went as we had hoped,
how it would be our history to know that the height of your
love for me was the day before you arrived in Ohio, the
day before this trial began. But I, instead, began to read the
nutritional facts about those Egg McMuffins, which were
printed so nicely on the packaging. For the first time in
seven months, I had sadly awakened to the hard
real facts: 300 calories per serving; 250 mg of cholesterol,
or the 12 g fat content, and the carbs. Jesus Christ! How did
I miss this? Why did it take so long for me to read this?

People make bad decisions every day. New lovers come at
it every time, lean and mean, forecasting only the good
ingredients, as those that will ultimately comprise the whole.

I picked up that firmly placed cup and sipped up
some orange juice, saying only—as I looked deeply
for the last time, into your Irish brown eyes …

Utah sure is beautiful. Who would have known
about any of this?

The Open Road

for my brother Rick

Each minute of your life begins as an excise tax,
each day, a note of more unreliable currency,
about which you come to understand little.
Each day of your life hangs out like waving
laundry on some country acreage where
lonesome truckers drive by at night and mistake
your white T-shirt for a sign that their own
life has gone too far or not nearly far enough.
Either way, they reach out on their CB for a copy,
but no one copies that, and the open road just widens.

The neighbors notice a light that won't go out
and which in turn indicates meaning in the bedroom.
They discuss the matter night after night,
year after year, as their own love lamp gets snuffed—
candle-like—until what gets left is the campfire
leftovers of pale gray smoke conspiring slowly
and mercilessly against gravity—more symbolism
in the heart of nothing. And what about you?

You recall your last hour of happiness as one in which
daylight was not a part. It was August, late in the month.
You knew she would leave in the morning, soft kiss,
an exit, a kiss full of knowledge and uncertainty. You
were too young for that kind of a thing, which only means,
in retrospect, love burns out in youth, though it doesn't
go quietly into the night. It rages and crackles into
oranges and fields of bedeviled burning beauty. Sure,

you make more of it now because later in life, it's
the painful routine of work and cerebral hours of rote sex
that haunt your evenings, and you know there's
no soft kiss coming, just an open-ended exit wound.

Clearly some window is still open. You ask yourself why, but
no one seems much longer to respond
    to these kinds of things.
Looking down and onto the scene, you hear a semi roaring
from at least a mile in advance as you take a seat in front
of your bedroom window, where a light breeze reminds your
senses about something that once took place in your life.
Maybe you're a trucker, maybe you're a white T-shirt
flagging down the enemy to say, "This is it, I'm out!"
Maybe the open road and its moonglow highway are
out there, steering you somewhere, saying, *Breaker 1-9,*
Country Flaps headed straight through
    Ghost Town; anyone copy?

But no one ever does, and the open road

just widens a little more.

Upon My Father's Advice

He said,
"Get in there and drink down the bottle
until the bottle means more than you."

He said,
"Get in here and sink through this bottle
until the bottle rises up through you."

He said,
"Get out of here and look into that mirror
until your face displaced is your every living fear."

He said,
"So here you go, son;
don't slow down through the bottle
up to the neck.
Lock it in tight,
and tonight, swing off,
right into everything your life is afraid to choose."

He said,
"Hang in there, son. Death is just around the noose."

"I would go there, son, around the noose.
I would go there if I, my son, were you."

The Lesson of a Circle

for my grandmother

It wasn't enough that I master
tying my own shoes by age four.
My brother had to tease me with the
double knot,
which I could not let go of
until it was securely bowed,
one, two, atop both of my shoes.

Early days. A smile and my summer shoes,
footing over twigs and now forgotten paths—
our routes, which enabled our
innocent souls to employ happiness
nearly each and every hour of the day.

The innate ability not to remember a damn thing:
where we'd been, who we'd been with,
or how long since sunrise—
and now, pinlight stars flecking a sky.

I imagine old age is the second version
of this kind of mysterious recess.

I wheel my grandmother down for
dinner at five. The nurses report
she's a quick study, and the therapy
is all putting her on target to go
home soon and relax her heart.

She tries, but I slowly insist—as
I carefully place her tiny gray shoe
over her white sock and I gently
double-knot both the right and left
shoe—you showed this all to me once,
the hold and slow twirl of it all,
the subtle tug of the experts.
You let me remind you how a
circle works, how it always comes
back to thank you in the end.

There, now we go to dinner.

The Inward Take

for SLD

The inward take of premium scotch
whisky placed

against the white throw of winter's best.
Miles of cold ancient weather
gathering up around you. This one

homemade cigarette fueling the
heart of song that will too soon
end,

and the wind will before your eyes
bring spring: a brightness, blinding
off the residue, removing this night,

the one, now, you recall, as you recall
your best-lost lover: the truest of spirits,
the strike of her kiss. Tonight, memory

is beautiful, and even in the cold, it's
nothing for you to remember her warmth,
as distant as it is.

The History Channel

Seven years was now the distance between us.
Our lives no more connected than a cut
cable or an old and buried telephone call.

Time is a serious warrior. Each of us has
our story, how it went down, or
less clearly, why it went down in flames.

It's always a Sunday when the past finds
you in crawl spaces, in attics, or unfinished
basements, where you open old wounds
of boxed secrets and spent timelines
as if you are opening up sadness for
the first time in your life. You become
some kind of anxious pirate unlocking
a hopeless chest of retired meaning.

Twelve microcassettes of raw footage sat
there, open-boxed, like a caught trout,
not knowing its true role, waiting for the fisherman
to make his move. You are amazed to find
what degree of care was taken to stow
away these personal claims.

You'll ask yourself in old age if the youth
of today still kiss with their hearts, and
do they fall frail when nothing comes
back from the final casting.

The man went on to live his life in obscurity.
The woman found out life can be held.

And still, he watches the raw footage as if
the History Channel has called up their story
as its main event, a must-see story of
a lifetime, one no one can live without.

Effortless Bliss of Life

for my grandmother

At some point, you will fail to collect that
	shadow of a lightning bug.
You will feel removed and feel measured
	as if the touchable world
has altogether quietly dismissed itself from
	your imagined table of life.

The bruised or forgotten fruits of your labor
	will no longer support you.
Faces and histories, those fortunate kisses and those hurting
hearts—not yet fully expressed—will pass
	dubiously, forever out of focus.

This is not to scare you, to place too
	much pain in the foreground.

At some point, love's brand of both time
	and space will occupy you.
You will take on assumed powers of
	those lost gods of cloud-filled
faces of wonderment and a designed
	intent of guiltless optimism.

A pair of freshly showered warm lips
	will dilute you, though only
later in the season or year, as you watch
	from an unsafe distance
as you guess how it used to be (once) to sync your kiss
of a supposed destiny with someone whose
	hope for you is not yet dead.

I want you to feel good about this, to dismiss
     the backdrop when necessary.

You see, just over the fading sounds of that horn,
just beyond the last ash of your best burned bridge,
just beneath the unqualified feelings you keep seeking
is a mossy set of cobblestone steps set temporarily solid.

Now, with each aching gesture upward, your silence will call
out everything it needs. Each following advancement
gives way to fewer errors, counters your
     worry with contradictions
of a believable mystery and a quantifiable peace:
It's just the heart's evolution, reaching peak for the last time,
releasing all five senses, and encountering
     the effortless bliss of life.

The Day My Son Left Me for College

for my mother

Fifteen years down the line, and finally,
she offered this one final observation:

I think college screwed you up.

Her sense that what Plato has
to offer is not of the heart,
and when you think Socrates is
helping make the case,
really, you're just working harder
toward removing yourself from
something bigger in the universe.

Where once she took pride in my
endless Dean's List postcards,
which were sent at the end of
each term, she had, I believe,
come to regret each and every one.

Citing my visceral tone and my
penchant for beating down the
opponent with broad strokes
until he's weakened. And then,
the final knockout: a world-class
pounding of verbs and adjectives,
each fast-tracking
the other into submission …

As a teen, she used to report,
he was kind and seemed most
interested in the good of people.
True, he wore his heart on his
sleeve, but after the education,
I barely saw his heart at all.

Left wondering, I suppose,
with a fair amount of
pain and grief, if those books
and tests took her boy, not
into an expanded world of
profound thought, but rather,
into distant and calculated
states of mind, quite nuclear
and negligible, ones in which
the learned are by comparison
far more stupid than any of
the ignorant, whom they
profess to ambitiously reject.

Song for Daryl

When your operating system cannot support itself,
and when it begins only to process binary threads of sadness,
things tend to get worse. People tag you as if you
are some endangered bird to be studied and written about.

They work out the finances and double down on
the opportunity to do everything but lose you entirely.

They call them homes, whether for old people or
for those of us whose operating system has met
capacity and cannot appropriately fulfill some
life requests adequately: a higher education, a job
application, or the ability to articulate and defend
ourselves in the face of a generally inhuman public.

The obligatory pickups and drop-offs that take place
around any given holiday. An allocated space
that serves to cut out some guilt of conscience.

Nothing here remotely close. Love becomes an awkward
gesture—the hug, the kiss, the smile—all out of range and
out of tune. My paradigm is that of a near-non-entity.
How sadly trapped I am as a man. To understand
just enough—that I am no more wanted in their lives
than a terminal illness or fractured tibia—something
broken or misunderstood. At any rate, it's everything
that equals loss in the world.

Once a young man came to visit me. He took the time.
We sat and listened to music, and he watched me
cry with happiness because music is truly holy and
above the merciless crimes of man and his condition.
He asked me about life, and I think he learned my
philosophy. Life, I cried with a smile, is when a
stranger walks into your room and gently turns your
wheelchair so that you can reach the volume and
turn up the beauty of music. Life, I said, is when
a human forgets to pity you and instead just
holds your hand and listens as if each breath of
life's distinction between us is lost and found
and held under the laws of melody, music, and kindness.
Nothing more, nothing less. A Song for Daryl
is what he called it, and it plays without delay,
always, throughout the course of my years.

Skein

My last working memory of it once and again
passes over me
like a skein of geese, just enough hint in the distance
to stop me, so that I set down my life
and pick up on the visual.

1977: Carter begins his socialist agenda.
1977: My father begins to systematically gut out his own
home country. A kind of redistribution of fists
and beatings and hard liquor begins;
no sumptuary laws in place to stop this
patriarchal course of killing off our gray matter.

When you are thirty, unmarried, and without children,
you hear more clearly that skein of geese
because your life you see flying in that
    V, its history and future,
its unknown centuries of battles and defense,
all trying to unlearn the very sky through which
you must meet yourself, through which you must
go in order to survive.

1979: The exiled Ayatollah Khomeini works his people up
so that hate for America becomes the full order of the day.
Then the US-backed Shah arrives on our
soil for cancer treatment. Those years, during my
father's rule, there were no available sanctions,
no OPECesque embargo to suppress our fearless father;
nothing, it seemed, to stop his home rule.

Time is now dead. There are no more working
memories, personal histories, or killing off of
gray matter. There is no more matter,
only when the world clicks on its axis for one
segmented second, a skein of geese passing
over me, just a hint in the distance so that
I put down my life like those militants put
down their guns, and we all for a temporal
minute just breathe and pick up the visual
particulars of peace, knowing that despite our

inhumanity, history has us now.

Pieces

Three objects rest on one golden placemat
made of white feathers and immeasurable fiction.

A gun, a plastic saint, and a sketch pad
dated from the early 1930s. Ask yourself,
How did any of this come to be?

Aunt Miriam was a drunk, sure,
no question about that,
but still, that satellite imagery and rare nude
footage of bullet and torn breast—well—
I'm at a distance on this one; can't quite say.
To declare any of it evidence strips its essence
of the minor decency here deserved, don't you think?

Look down the goddamn river, for Christ's sake—
the fog, not the lily pad, nor the dopey carp
playing possum for bread, nor the turtle's imprint.
No, I say, look down the goddamn barrel
and retrace the bold blue behavior you set upon this table.

He's a practicing Catholic, isn't he? I said, isn't he?
Motherfucker, quiet and peaceable, until the rapist
living in his large toe wakes full-scale, mid-morning,
searching for low-hanging fruit. Oh, and here comes you.

Hand me my 4B charcoal pencil. I got a few things
to display. It's a secret, isn't it? Goddamn you.
Set still; do not move a muscle, or I swear to life,
I'll command this saint to sketch you being shot

Dead!

Out of Phase

And it comes to this,
dried and pressed roses,

red ash—

The stowed-away (hidden, really)
letters about how neither of us
could stand another earthly minute
apart from the other.

Cloud rides through the ancient
atmosphere: you to my Ohio;
me landing in your city where natives
tug morning lemons from a front
tree lodged in a ground of history.

Were it not for this medication and
its subsequent deferment of more
crystallized emotions, one imagines
I could easily be drawn into tears
as head down upon the placemat
of our history.

Not only this, but so many
other careful and wonderful losses.

We are both getting on, absent the
home and children, those we once
in a San Francisco cafe discussed,
like an Alcatrazian break: We'd split

for a new life, survive the harsh
waters and odds, come up with
something for which we'd both be
proud, never to be desperate or
without again.

Be well, I know you will.

I am forgotten now. The storms have
all passed. Look, a rainbow delays its
temporal metaphorical memorial of
magic, for you and for me.
We are so very lucky to have caused it,
held briefly onto it, and then prayed below
its bent meaning, one side to the
next, never again, its beginning and
ending are finally—as are we—
out of phase.

Message from My Father

You want so badly to enable the part of me that loves.

Ghosts, the residual resolute diatribes that won't
turn off their internal voices. And so we listen
as if we are in the tomb of their bodily mindspeak.

My father, oh father, twenty-one years now. Your
voice is all cobblestone and deteriorating flesh-lung,
walking or crying toward me:

Son, it's your father. If you get a chance,
call me tomorrow. Thank you.

Thirty-two years, I assumed your love, its reach,
the strong throttle of your manly voice, which
controlled each and every arm of the family soul.

But the crying has all but come to an end.

Please leave no more messages—the awareness
too strong upon my vital signs, not enough
courage to surpass any angst I have so long known.

Take care, bury the past with your heart, and
know that your son can no longer receive.
Perhaps our world is now a shadow, and you
its blank space, abandoned, unknown and lost.

Matryoshka

Beyond this one empty box (box #1), whose own
life is only viewed as plotted land, tax revenue, and a
sum-total line-item on some insurer's general ledger,
there are only strangers called neighbors; words we
use to artificially enhance the relationship—a sort of
Splenda sprinkled generously across property lines.

During our lives, some of them will deed a smaller
or larger box, accompanied by a garage (box #2).

Now, as for box #3, the one on four wheels—the
"transport enabler," as I like to call it. Estimates say
nearly sixteen million Model Ts were purchased in the
United States during this car's life. This box allows
us to (in our own way) defeat time—that is, cover
more square footage in our lives than we otherwise
might, were we without our transport enablers. We
continue to build them, refine them: faster and so on.

Some days when the work day has gone on for too
long and my own personal aversion to humans has
grown ever stronger, I pull up in box #1's driveway,
leave box #3 running in front of box #2, and I
begin to question longhand in my mind, the things
that have gone horribly wrong in my life.
My memory coaxes me back to 1977, a sun-spilled
day when strangers-called-neighbors discovered
a fifty-seven-year-old steelworker foreman locked inside
first, his box #2 and second, his box #3.

Box #3 was a 1958 Chevrolet Brookwood station wagon.
My grandfather, as its only owner, kept it in absolute mint
condition. It was Monday, July 4, 1977—a day of
celebration, independence, a day of newly found freedom.

I imagine Raymond's day had gone on for too long and his
own aversion to humans had grown
    resolute that day. The timeline
suggests two hours of hard drinking (usually Johnnie Walker)
at Fat's Pub before he pulled alongside and passed his box #1
and pulled his box #3 into his box #2. This
    is how life works sometimes,
for some people: matryoshka. Our lives
    as Russian nesting dolls.
There were an estimated 32,000 suicides in the United States
in 1977. How many were overworked and life-depleted
persons such as my grandfather, I cannot say. How many
drove 1958 Brookwoods shall remain a mystery to me. He
was a man with many more boxes: a wife, daughters, a son,
grandchildren, a brother, a mother and father, a life.

Raymond and I have a few things in common, though
as a seven-year-old, I couldn't have known that then.

All I am saying is that some days when the work day
has gone on for too long and my own personal aversion
to humans has grown ever stronger, I pull up in box #1's
driveway and leave box #3 running in front of box #2, and I
think about my grandfather, how he
    must have used shorthand
in thinking about how the things in his own life had gone
horribly wrong, and how sometimes there's no real need
to pause, only to continue on with how your life must end—

as a Russian nesting doll—one capsule placed inside the
other: a home, a car, a garage, a family, a career, all
evenly spaced into layers, until this one final body
and face rests on the exterior: You, placed gently into
box #4, the silk-laden carrier box, which whispers
in ghost-speak that reminds you why you are leaving
this place, that your layers, not one and not all, could
keep a man like you alive with any sense

of achievable purpose.

Martini Dreams

I walked along the sidewalk, and with
the beard of a homeless man,
feared life was worse than any death
imaginable. The pirates walked into
the nude and complacent areas,
where young women continued to
dance and frolic, in order to forget
their Midwest lives.

I came here seeking freedom. The sketch
of American happiness, an erasure
cleared upon, maybe a forest, one
in which the natives are called into question.
What is not normal must be destroyed.

The canoe was left waiting for me. I drew
carefully upon the echo of the mountain's
resolve, which was a full landscape
over the river body, and reverence;
I peddled evenly and with conviction,
as if each minor stroke played a major
part in my future history as a person.

Cannibals mocked my travels. The miles
were ancient and uncalled for,
and time became my future transient, who,
left to its own argument, might have
killed me in the name of the Athenians,
accusing me of teachings unbecoming
of one who ought to live a world of silence.

And then my eyes took to the shore.
A figure waiting patiently. The sky cried
Godot. Indians from all nations piled
together and began to rewind their past—
white men in droves died by the tips
of poisonous arrows, repealed their
cause in a bullet-fumed remorse.

I climbed down to my knees to question reality.
Father, dear father, you killed
me when you left; life is our severance pay,
death nothing more than a calm
sunset answered, one whose pace is that
of a snail, pregnant and barely able to
stretch its heart-rind dreams across your

finish line, is where upon I last learned, I had
died.

Lost Summer

With age and the derivatives of each and every
lost summer
arrives a somber crush from reality—that your
life is somehow a little more exposed,
a little less of a secret or susceptible to wild
happenings—fever-pitch evenings of
highway sex and windblown rushes of
absolute
nothing to regret, to look forward to,
or to dismiss as simply happenstance.

The young-skinned zombies in your office
see you as
a sterile demographic: half moon, half
dying wolf, a portion of your own youth
bobbing weightlessly away until the water
covers over any signs that once you
were one of them: stupidly drunk and happy.

But there's hope. Okay, there is no hope.

It's all cliché, been done, you see.
This is the unbroken transfer of it all,
just how it is designed; the order you think
and talk about, this absolute measure
of our lives.

Believe in its elements. I don't say
revel in it; time may be
too terse for that kind of review.

But today,
the honey, the bees, the sweetness
remembered, is it now? Today

the lost summer is the prize. Reward
yourself; the sun may be closer than
you think, or the moon farther
away than that. Either way, there's
something listening for the distance,

the echo of a lost summer petitioning:
Come back! I'll love you this time around,
you silly little orbit, you.

You silly little orbit.

Hard Kiss

On the cusp of cutting off,
as a lost air wave,
you say loneliness is long and unforgivable.

Our Labor Day kiss. You lied. He knew.

Our embrace races down a dreamy
hill, maybe San Francisco's
Lombard Street, through the Telegraph Hill
neighborhoods, a soapbox derby car,
rickety, roars and reality snores,
and we take kite-flight, to suddenly
resolve our hurried pulses at Ghirardelli Square,

for coffee, and a refreshed sense about
how we could not morally make work
our love for one another. He knew.

I pressed out evenly each and every thought.

Our hard kissing, losing out to life's so-called
circumstances.
The shadow of leaves learning our pain, the
very insects looking up at our aging echoes,
and then burying themselves beneath the soil.

The dark resistance; without resistance,
my final space in your heart could have
gone missing forever.

I woke up bruised, inside of the N. C. Wyeth museum.
From saintly chocolate bites to a book shop at
Chadd's Ford. Newell, too, wanted more from his life
than illustrations—his means to an end, never able
to convert what's lucrative into that which satisfies.

Leaving the Kent State parking lot, the whole of me
was taken away. It happens on fall-fevered afternoons.
An old lover calls; you claim the clouds are your own,
but storms deliver a hard kiss in ways you cannot forget:

The truest fires are oftentimes left burning in your heart
forever.

Ghost and Hostage

The thought my father thought has not yet reached me.
He is not real, yet there are those who claim his flesh
is still among the living; but for me, his existence is dead.

I am being held hostage by a ghost. Its vaporous body
controls me—me, a deserted marionette left hanging,
waiting for my own Godot, which, it happens, never comes.

A swing, a kick, or a lost fist toss into the world's wind,
nothing to grab or pull or center and refocus upon;
no concrete person, place, or thing onto
    which I might fling myself,
impose force, work out some science or sense about.

What is there after killing? Death is an unresolved notion.
It does not acknowledge its bodies, its
    debris, its soundless souls.

Our lives sing their melodies beyond the bucket-soil graves.
Our lives hold their meaning in ways unattached to muscle
and bone, so that memory becomes the active and indelible
agent, so that actions and words are the only distributable
exponent, our only chance to raise the power and receive
the living in a way that doesn't disturb our fibrous mass.

I thought my father thought he had a son of some worth.
That is not real, yet there are some who believe in this
pot of gold, the lottery-ticket souls, the people who trade
currency for wishing wells and lighthouse dreams. But that
kind of foggy trust is dead to me; I am still among the living.

Fish (the one that got away)

I was too young, dumb for the thought.

I was too young, dumb for the thought,
so what did the thought do for me,
to have and hold and later be sold,

for the air that I thought could be bought,
borrowed and betrayed, silly and persuaded?

I was too young, dumb for the thought,
and she, she was the wiser, waiting for me
temporarily, to show me how enlightened life

could be, but not for me.
I was too young, dumb for the thought,
so the thought and she both have easily escaped me.

Easter Egg Picture

Were it not for this picture illustrating my undeniable
happiness as a child, no concrete evidence otherwise
suggests in the least a narrow or broad-landscaped
history of normalcy, of healthy growth, of a six-year-old
blond American kid from a small union town in Ohio.

Based on the evidence—a newly dyed Easter egg, orange
and blue with green swivel-stripes around its oval body—
my mother, brother, and myself act out a traditionally
American and quasi-Christian scene: Behold! the Easter egg.

It is only after thirty years of mental playback that I
consider who it is taking this picture and why that
person has gone missing from it. My mother reviews
it with me on my thirty-eighth birthday, confirming
my suspicion: It was our father who always took the pictures.

This would have been eighteen months before
he left us. There's no picture for that scene, exactly.

Since the development of this Kodak moment,
my mind has worried and become ill in its own nature.
The toll taken cannot be realized in a dark room
nor be digitally reproduced and pushed out to the
ether for extended family and strangers to find.

A day is coming in which humans will give up this physical
evidence—in its place, an untouchable digital universe.
Not so unlike my father, who must have known the day
would come to this. A man ahead of his time, knowing
that to be remiss is also to remain fully intact inside
the memory of others. You see, sometimes
    no picture is required.

Debt

The day, drawn out of existence and possibly against its will,
cuts the tether and thus separates last night's lean moon
from this curious full-bodied sunlight of
    an inescapable morning.

I find myself not only alone, but lonely, an unfamiliar context
into which I have been placed, and for reasons I cannot say.

It's possible, I suppose, that the heavens
    are readying themselves
to throw down three aces or a full house,
    something that might
force my hand by showing that I am
    without any winning cards.

I sit idle in front of a white and blinding screen,
penniless and obese, far more successful
    than one imagined possible,
yet lonely, like a lost cause or failed grade,
troubled by the very senses that I once used to convert
inklings into feelings or hunches into reliable conclusions.

At what stage of life does a desert face its own reality
that becoming an ocean is not possible, or having humans
swim across it, well, it's simply not a reasonable thought
to pursue, not only at this point but ever.

I'm in quicksand, it seems. It has me surrounded.
Those Boy Scout lessons I cannot recall—I remember
lungs: Keep them filled with air and breathe deeply.

This all helps one to remain buoyant—yes, buoyant
is just what I need. No need to be reckless or wave about
to such a degree my limbs lose energy, and then,
who knows? I'm in quicksand,

hoping for some action-hero resolve, but my eyes see
nothing out there, and far from any acoustic echoes
of any kind, I no longer hear a thing, cannot in fact,
feel this silt devilish brown monster that is swallowing
me whole, biting through my tongue, though cannot
define the blood, its origin, no taste whatsoever.
I have no sense of this situation, and my equilibrium
settles the debt: I am finally seconds from falling
off the grid, where I settle on the X and Y, where
the premise of my existence follows its conclusion to my

death. Yes, this settles it.

Cardiovert

for my grandmother

We have terms for these kinds of things
to cover the cost of our stopped hearts

when love or daytime TV or insatiable
sweets—upon which we depend
too much—
fail us outright and throw back lashes
of hellfire: a response, a rebuke, and then
a truthful silence.

The human life gets taken and given back
in time, in sync; we reply with our lives.

Please return my grandmother.

Do not say a word save:
keep silence to yourself.
Deliver back with words:

Her safety is yours again, in
full measure, her heart hurries to you!

We'll cry because the human parts
cannot always save us so directly.
Yet when they do, joy becomes the kiss
of earth, the reach to the center of our souls.

You know I love you; now come home.

The Diaphanous Glue

Here it is, before you,

the subtle structure of our lives,
the diaphanous glue—
barely sticking,
turning more transparent
and asthenic by the day.

You wake, eyes less clear
about the latest blue sky
or whiteout—the night
prior, when love itself
would not take, did not
give back, simply could
not release a thing.

For now, the many missed
understandings comfort,
like a boy lapped into
the very soul of a lamb,
or a man able to put down
his gun and hug effortlessly
his enemy, their shared
sacrificed pasts.

Tomorrow it will all be gone.
This spirit, that love, our
enemy abroad or next
door; but still, it will love,
be waking—renewing

itself as
the diaphanous glue—if barely
sticking, still enough hold,
to keep the hearts of many
holding this gloriously all
together now.

I Woke to Take a Walk

I woke to take a walk
that day.
The sun a sky the blue

rebirth of life
a step then step
to take a walk
that way,

heading out toward the last lumber's edge
of the dock,
where fish find their quarry light held

captive against a saintly voiceless air.
I care to know. I came to see the years

far behind me and their tears dried like
ancient figs.

Eyes still: the dark-eyed junco and the
Stellar's jay
collecting nutrient, balancing the subtle
cells of memory's brink …

Of their being on the crest of a heron's
departure, somewhere in Ohio, where

I spoke the words I wrote
that night.
Our moon the sky the great

widening,
which I trust
is not a divide, but is something
other than the thing itself,
undeniable and waterproofed for truth.

This Far

Place your plum face with its eyes closed into the fair
breeze of a closing day, and try to cope for a moment
when you cannot see how humanity has made it this far.

Arrange in your mind, with its abstract expressions, a
kiss coming from across the way. Now lean for a minute
inward as the brick-and-mortar days try to unsteady you.

Learn to convert, where the parallel of photosynthesis
demands it, that where once no energy ran, now the birds
and plush lawn and oak leaves and earth-top might
fill in the many hardened voids accrued through sadness.

Leave this space and fly into the good evening of your
heart such that all pressed and repressed senses
scatter free and skip seasons to replenish the cost
of hurt and bent and bruised and overused feelings.

If I say this too simply, then you'll receive it more easily.

Place your plum face with its eyes closed into the fair
breeze of a closing day, and try to cope for a moment
when you cannot conceive how humanity
    has made it this far.

Open to New Things

What man so easily sours on his life as if ten thousand
lemons alone should be a deal breaker?

Why not hold strong, through to the next inning or
quarter or business meeting, where certain chances
are sure to present themselves?

The art of it all is perseverance. This I say with
certainty and with a fair number of evaluated
failures to my credit: women, jobs, the whole lot.

Do not be so ready to always so quickly
court the end of a kiss or a real punch in
the face. There are lessons to be turned
and nurtured and ultimately harvested.

And while the end of everything is a certainty,
the beginning of each new nothing can be,
if you will only allow, a triumphant
and unexpected joy of inane singular fits
and seizures, ready to exact your very
body and mind into a walking coma.

Why aren't you willing to be more
open to new things? Why?

On Any Afternoon

Where the rose does not bloom, or the
    heart widen any afternoon,
you'll find a life-chance anew—the truest
    moment in a series of falsities.

It is much too easy (you see) to kneel and
    settle alongside the dead.
The challenge in living is to rise steadily
    and walk in a world of life.

Get to the symmetry. Allow this geometry, its
    lines and points, its exceptional
intersections, to unravel and necessarily connect
    that which needs to be attached.

The ligaments and bones have no opinion
    on the matter. Oh, but the soul, it
is the preacher and pulpit, the apolitical
    proposition of our very existence.

Collect its voice—this butterfly of all
    reason. And then let it sing until
your life fills with a kind of hearing, a full
    encounter with a complete melody,
where the rose must always bloom, and the
    heart widen on any afternoon.

Nature's Holy Cure

I awoke
with a marked sadness splitting my human vine,
somewhere between my potential and my weaknesses.

The fields of my existence—I looked out
over them to consider the climate against the day.
The sun was expanding—a yellow tumor above it all.

To the west, a sworn secrecy. The river contradicts this,
in blues and whitewater grays, its snaking shifts,
allowing me little in the way of a purified knowledge.

I couldn't bring myself to think about love, its handling.
I just kept driving through the spirit of what was happening
to me—umbilical cord being reassigned to a new life.

As I ascended north, the mountains turned into a wide
quiet choir of roughly one hundred thousand singing
tombstones, their forgiving voices paging out to me,
an invitation, really, to place myself toward the sky,
begin to release resistance, and simply free-fall from it all.

This reminds me of when I was a boy, my mother would
arrive at my bed. Knowing I had been crying, though not
clear on why,
she would tuck me into her motherly hug to hold
onto the boy she was losing, the man she knew
wouldn't turn up right one day, or at least that's how it felt,
as the boy cried into her worn-out shirtsleeve.

By the time I had peaked, the rivers below were feasting
and collecting the remnants of yesterday's news,
passing on the time, paying no mind
    about such marked sadness.

Maybe nature has a more holy cure in
    ignoring its weaknesses,
knowing they will all in time detach, dissolve, and be
made like so much of the living—not even
    a memory here anymore.
Likened to a wind-split of leaf from its branch, nutrient from
its soul, just a common sense approach
    to an unwanted disposition.

In the Minute

If in the minute your life takes over, it all
running
wild, and bones stricken, no, shocked
out of their calcium, man, I aim to
say, if in the minute
there's no replay or reply about
how in the world you stand

as a man in the minute of a world
before the punch and puke and
oral rebuke of the sun striking
over the sunburned hours of limitless
misfortune, no, scorching
rivers raging red, ablaze, man,
I aim to say, in the minute
you choose not to lose it all,

running
wild, and bones stricken, no, shocked
into the bodily system that is you,
you choose, you have, you've chosen,
and among the few: now, you are

in the minute.

How Light Joins the Birds

The light joins the birds inside of our winter turndown
to walk the paths in memory,
filled with brush-faced, full leaves of
day, twigs, and morning earth,

and our future standing in wait, as in a trained connection.

What links the sun to the juniper, the man to his
bedeviled season of white cold, or a woman
to her failed body parts, whose soul is left whole?

I take a look,
spy the book, and surprised by further scansion,
alone, discover I am with it all:

the woman, the hawk, the soil, the linked
progression of world and words united.

Dormant for a time—but yes, waiting
in a patient station, a hub, a drifter's paradise.

We will, I dare say, connect, get together,
and move—as with all seasons to come—this
motive along its tracks until an accurate
destination spills us off for further examination.

Artful Impression

You must endure through the many doors
    of pain and inexcusable
actions in order to know for sure that your
    own are unequivocally just.

The mirrors merely will not be enough—
    light echoes or drifting
shadows of subtly moon-full evenings:
    What if they are suspect?

Years of conversation—the derelict
    priest, the sad boss, or with
old lovers who no more recall what is true than you do.

Go out and into yourself. Forge the new
    molecules, strengthen
the twin synapses, such that all within
    you becomes triumphant.

You must secure through the newly
    drawn doors an art and fate
that will close behind it—without fail—
    all prior versions of self.

Go the greater distance, beyond the average hum, and learn
how a future gets born, without destiny,
    rather, by our means alone.

A Riot in My Mind

There is a riot in my mind,
a pendulum timed
about the swinging distance
surveying both cause and control.

Along the atmosphere
a fear, both vertical and long,
a trap for bear fat and wild hog song.

Someone has set this test with
intentions and perfectly sprung
denials, left like a summer desire.

I must creep away, no more force
than that of a hovering ant, lest
I go snapped-back, and into the
reverse portal of my own heart.

Behind the Fault Line

What causes a man not to be lonely
for a woman, a career, or a chance to
be a part of those things?

It's a strange condition in a world
or city or country in which makeshift
lives waver and build themselves
unwittingly along fault lines, lines
whose tremors divide fact from fiction,
and whose sudden quakes alert
bystanders to stay far behind the line.

I see them holding hands and climbing
ladders—perfectly faked mannerisms
galore, exchanging data and mucus,
sleeping and responding like androids.
I think it must be a fairly flickery existence.
Stem cell research should help get these
molecules and atoms into their proper
containers the first time; avoid the missteps
and clue the 'droids into what gets things
exact the first time—the lover, the job.

Meanwhile, back at the homestead, I plan
an evening of Art Blakey, self-love, and
a new crab quiche recipe from an old,
old flame. She always sends her love, and
that goes a long way; at least it keeps me
behind the line, away from the faults, and

nearer to a ladder I can climb, a love I
can handle (for better or for worse), and away
from the equivocal data and mucus of all modern man.

Á la vôtre!

Beyond the Pop Song

It happens as the augmented chord goes
    jazz into a lazy Saturday night.
You reach for happiness, but top-shelf is three higher than
the place that can get you half the distance,
    and that's all you really can afford.

Bill Evans delivers, "The Two Lonely People"
    plays on the piano, rivers
judiciously back and forth; a coda that will not
    quit you, a syllable— ruby red and
repeated—until its kiss gets you off the
    atmosphere and into something more
comfortable.

A wild-eyed cocktail, cold and alarming,
    but easy; through the eyes of
middle-aged mementos, locked shoeboxes,
    and women that warn you,
life ticks on their watch; so watch it, and do
    not—whatever you do *do*—be late.

It happens when the tritone substitutions
    go missing, leaving your minor
chord without an accomplice. I see it this way
    every time I make the mistake.
Love, crying and screaming, time getting even
    as sorrow swan dives up from its abyss.

Lester Young looms on his horn, as if black
    and white finally meet equal,
and the only enemy is the predictable politician,
    the cheating husband and wife,
or the naked maid that placates judgment in
    place of a perfectly fitted dollar bill.

It's everything from which I have learned to
    run. To run from it is all I know to do.
Whether it's you or you or you: you all strike
    me wrongly as helplessly tonal.

And so it happens when the augmented chord
    makes jazz out of a lazy Saturday night—
my polyrhythmic fantasy that love itself may
    one day move beyond the pop song.

The Evidence of Demarcation

for SCR

The evidence against our never knowing true
    creation rests in our existence.
(Was that a question or was that your
    answer? I am uncertain. Thanks.)

Our brevity with circuitry lobes split like
    cantaloupes helps us pass the time.

It's telephony personified, the true and
    tried method of triangulation:
three points meeting in space to say, "Hey,
    you have a new voice mail!"
(Where? Down there. Why? Because.
    Who? Don't know yet. Thanks.)

Soon the vagina, like the eagle and salmon, will be brought
into their series circuit: all current relegated
    through all components,
the sum of each feeling creating a total resistance,
though without a breaker. And as each
    primal feeling goes out,
the broken circuit will be monitored for
    use in their final conversion.

And the evidence against our never knowing
    true creation rests in our existence.

Our molecular obsession with the leukotomy
	by Moniz et al. has transferred
to higher scholarly aspirations. What
	say we cyborg for a while?
We treat it all as if we humans—beating hearts
	and all—are the twenty-first century's
answer to spinsterdom, all of us sitting
	pitifully with barren dance cards.
(What about me? What about you? Can't I
	dance? Don't know yet. Thanks.)

The speed and severity are vaporous to you all.
The need and disparity are too numerous to recall,
this parasitic rage, our science hijacked by the new
elecborg government: absolute power by many
of the most unenlightened magna cum laudes
you'll ever be forced against. It's a war, to be sure.

The electric curriculum has come aboard, and with it,
professors and fully informed administrators, the
backpack of the elecborg government's Swiss knife.

Now, the existence in our creation isn't the
	evidence for our true knowing.
(How can you say this? I must. Who are
	you? I am you. Why? Thanks.)

Take this last sentence and go.
(Where is it? Forthcoming. Soon? Yes. Okay, thanks.)

Trust no one, which means the fully
	ignorant, the widely educated,
and most certainly the average and in-between.

The evidence of demarcation is absolute yet invisible. Got it?
(Was that the one? Yes. The sentence,
    I mean? Yes. Okay, thanks,
and I must say, you seem like a real pal.
    I'm not. Oh, okay, thanks.)

Valley of the Deer

Embark here upon an evening with Glenfiddich.
Sip the scotch—which zings upon the tongue,
sparks and barrels of dried summer pears, all
ablaze into a crackling color of ancient oranges
and filled in with a palatable history of reprise.

Stay only for the moment memory.

Your small suburban castle is table set for one:
one meal, one tumbler of water, and one
perfect scotch glass filled in with this
gold molasses Gaelic fuel; twelve years,
now freedom breathes up, out, and back in.

The volume and glass are raised equally
high, and Johannes strides his strings
into the naked aisle of one final thought.

Here we are: running wildly in the
Valley of the Deer. Only the elegant notes
of fresh pear and subtle oak between us.

To Wait, Beyond

You wait, beyond.

Now the TVs are off, the belligerent sound of your
neighbor's kids disappears. The late night turns
into a knowable whisper.

Stout and freedom. Alone is a kind place
to be. No other half to inform you, to adjudicate
over this stately domestic silence.

No phones, too late to call, even the sex
lines are no longer receiving.

No supervisor blathering idiocy—the kind that
takes too long in its world echo to disappear
completely.

You settle to the piano, define root and harmony
through dead air, of night and star, of a cooling
space—just light enough to articulate
shadow, frame the very caricature of
nuisance: chord down softly, as the moon
hums electric, and you wait, beyond,

as it all plays itself out.

Where the River Keeps No Gods

"Go! Go! Go! I'll meet up with you where the river keeps
no gods." Forgive me, that's what Pastor Ken used to say.
He never explained it, of all things …

No, no, no,
it simply cannot be midnight already,
or I've already walked again, too far, in
  the wrong direction. I am
swearing this to you, that I saw Vladimir; he too now knows
how wrong and unreasonable he's been. But there's more.

I overheard you quote that dead Chicago lawyer-turned-poet,
something about: people never say the truth directly in
front of our eyes; they wait to be penned
  into some anthology—
a situation in which the author takes
  over and, reliably as he can,
tells everyone who they really are and
  what others really think
of them. He said you said I am a liar, though that in no way
diminishes your love for me. It's just a
  fact, so he said it like that.

By the way, Willy called. He's in Boston;
  things are going great.
This time, I think he's really making an
  appearance, you know,
within the business world. He's creating
  some real personal interest,
and so I know this time he's really going
  to make good. It's obvious.

You keep looking, but I can't see
or hear you any longer. Your words upon
    the earth remind me of
nothing. Why have our hearts changed so?

Before we're born again, I guess we should
    get a few things straight.
Love will always be misguided; and humans
    are built with ill direction
in their hearts and minds. They do love,
    but they also kill and regret
and summarize their losses within their
    respective abilities to forget.
Please forget how grand of a failure I've
    become. Don't count the losses.

I hope I never forget this earth, the way
    your eyes lovingly brutalized
my existence; the manner in which your
    skin overtook time so that
I could no longer track it, for better or for
    worse. This is only a summary,
a caption on the page or a blue dot lost
    in heaven. Either way, I am
saying with it, goodbye. Don't look any longer
    than you need to. Remember,

I'll meet you where the river keeps no gods.
    There, faith and fortune might
wed our souls and drive home the curious
    cause of existence as if they are
as simple as a sunset where the wealthy
    laugh and the poor just burn away.

Extended Offerings

The Story of My Friend Bai

Oh sins still do run spine-and-child through
    the now-dried dirt rivers of my years.
The Chinese neighbor boy, that brick screaming
    too hard in love with gravity
that did land itself against his supple head.

My summer memoir
here each of my seven years
unlocked using combinations
I might never truly understand.

The terror and his tears, his blood and his fears
exploited outright. What went wrong was everything.

Thundering metal cars, iron aliens we dubbed them—
storming locomotive
through our backyards before dinner time, the
temporal gifts boys spoiled themselves with
when baseball and moving targets were our only concern.

Bah-doong! Boof! Tah-ting!
Then laughter from Kurt: "I got it, Cliffy, I hit
    number seven twice … *twice*!"

"Watch this one, Kurt."

But, you see, it's thirty-nine years later. I
    am just now learning to grow

old, and in between losing my love of
    family, my taste for fine foods,
or the meager career I copy and paste
day in and year out, something here
in my heart awakens
a pain unmanaged
a thoroughfare now open
a part of my history left standing
ache-naked inside my mind's telegraph.

Bai (he used to say, bah-hee, that's me).

Bai. His was the only foreign family in our neighborhood,
1970s suburbia, Ohio, where innocence
    and boyhood friendship
linked together like two or three or four
    perfectly connected train cars.

Those rocks were fresh from a quarry four cities north of us.

I remember how sun-spoiled was our evening
    before it all turned into pure hellfire.
What went wrong was everything.
If you live long enough,
you learn every goddamn thing
in this life is known to do exactly that.

It was me proving my strength over Kurt, Jimmy,
    and Robert. But where was Bai?
The train soaring and firing itself off through space
like a thousand war cannons in our ears,
ferocious sounds: "Werrrrr, shuck, shuck, shuck,
    shuck … vooooooooom, werrrrr,
shuck, shuck, shuck …"

I spotted it among the rocks, large, heavy,
    an immaculate solid red.

The vacuum causation of it all. Madness. The lift, the full turn
and then

the release of the red brick
slow
flower-flight upon what movie played in my mind
of erratic energies now absent from
    this still life, I do not know.

We raised our boy hands like marching band
cymbals to cover our ears
amidst the chaos of confused neighbors
collecting and exchanging information.
What exactly happened here?

The anger exposed was so important and serious. It
    scared me that a man could force his own pain back
    into me: "God will never forgive this!" His father kept
    screaming this repeatedly, once in English followed by
    Chinese, until his vacillating cadence brought about
    my first memory of shame and sadness unified.

For me, one of the eerie and more powerful attributions
    of human existence is our not knowing what exactly
    ties one experience, memory, or thought to another.
    Once the objective qualifications of being human are
    met, we are left with only the subjective knowing, so to
    speak, about every minute, month, or year of our lives.

The year following this awful accident in which my friend
    Bai might have died due to my childhood negligence, my

father sold our house, divorced our mother, and took with him our savings, our new car, and any one cent we might have used to survive. What he did leave was a kind of change imposed upon me that has affected me my entire life. It is only after nearly forty years of absence that this summer memory has resurfaced in a way I never might have otherwise considered. Is there truth to be measured in each deed, intentional or otherwise, in a person's life? Certainly my father knew in his own mind the trajectory of my and my brother's life, not to mention his wife, once he systematically removed himself as husband, father, and breadwinner. His was no accident. Clearly his record now shows he was inspired and motivated by careful planning and with an intent to harm. But I meant no such harm to my young friend Bai. We were young boys throwing rocks at a train, pretending each of us to be Jim Palmer throwing his favorite pitch, the fastball, away.

There was nothing more to be done after the accident. The neighbors slowly dissolved back into their homes, the ambulance took Bai to the hospital, and the Choi family never let me apologize to them or their son.

There was nothing more to be done after my father left. Both sons and their mother dissolved, but not back to their home on Meadow Brook Lane. Everything had changed. What connection, if any, there is between my actions that summer day and my father's one year later I cannot say.

What I do tend to believe is what Mr. Choi could not stop himself from reiterating as he waved and pointed at me that day: "God will never forgive this!"

And it's true, He has not.

Fighting Time

I am fighting nothing beyond the margins
of time, this time as a segment within the largest
sorrows burrowed
like thieves on the run
or newly sprung bunnies
from an
overly thatched summer lawn.

The discovery phase feels in reverse,
strangely left unattended. It appears
information is in arrears, and I cannot
shift my assumptions,
get to the conclusion
at will.

I agree, someone ought to
check into this.

If he were still a boy, not just any boy …
Still a kid from the old block once
ran two miles to tell his mother
there'd been an irreversible accident.
Everyone favored that kid, but it
didn't last.

Too much of this life is unavoidable.
Young boys, their courage at stake
against an exhausting summer sun
falling into its own deep sleep,
the four of us standing like

a set of dumb second cousins,
our decisions no longer linked.
All things systematically detached.
We counted down over the water
from the rusty train trestle.

We counted on fear getting lost,
if only for a second; it did.
I'll still be damned
decades later,
heads first, if guts were not your shortcoming. Forty feet,
    gravity in check, off we went into the wonderful
    nonsense of boyhood at a glance: all risk with no
    mention of common sense, good judgment, or
    the thought that young flesh tears just as easily
    as old flesh; and the head easier than that.

Splash!

Blood under water,
body fighting time.
Kurt's boy heart alert
and tracking fate with each new step
homebound and raw with a pure and accelerated
sense of both life and death equally.

What was human necessity that day?
The lie, self-preservation, the thrill of assuming
he too would be okay?

Luck is a bitch if you have none. Life is even worse.
So watch how deep you're willing
into the murky world to jump

headfirst,
eyes closed,
and limbs lastly
swingin' sun down off the dead-end trestle
of your choice.

Joy

I guess you knew
but for the fear that can arrive
like nobody's business
or a T-bone collision
that turns steel into
a softened accordion of remorse.

Cry
because not all is pain
or severance
because
when you dig deep
you find your soul.

Joy.

Winter's Spacing

Consider love out of the question.
Couplehood over time equals just such a notion.

Any heart's contusion—nothing breaks exactly,
though bruises over time get a man or woman thinking.

I don't agree with our spacing; it's become a bit much.
Too thin is the line that divides us now.

What in the winter are we doing here?

Dead air, trunks and branches,
a landscape gone missing—
the hooded warbler heart,
the descending scream
of a red-tailed hawk securing nutrient,
or that private temporal prize
discovered right over there last summer,
a young nest of baby rabbits.
They only stayed for three weeks,
but my heart, as with you, holds
up a different version of time:
How loss always stays with me.

But then, we've lived to expect this
cyclic unknowing of universal sprocket-turning,
our days subject to changes:
tilt of the axis, orbital variation—the sidereal day.
They call it the nebula collapsing—a loss of momentum.

I feel it when it happens; maybe you do, too.
Our human blood slowing or thinning, losing
exactitude so that normal circulation is out of the question.
And yet, no one can say for certain when love may
or may not be cyclic, changed, or taken
  out as variable forever.

What I do know, what I do say to you:
Ah, spring, you soft yellow devil,
riding out to historic horizons and depths,
leaving us to face each other without the benefit
of an oak tree filled out, a lush, wet green
  lawn beneath a sunset,
or hope. And it's the hope we cling to as the seasons
divide and as lovers free themselves from
  all that change cannot keep.

Silent Parade

After the final vote,
council concluded its history be forgotten.
Here this year our town's
parade would for once throw out
no candy to waiting children, no foghorn-blowing clowns
circling in backyard-built go-carts.
No horns whatever were to be blown
from beneath the hoods of antique cars,
and certainly nary an amplifier or microphone was
to be injected into the silence of this proposed day:

Heretofore known as the Silent Parade.
(Yes, here was the plan!)

Taking lead position was our very own
    high school marching band.
Now, all horn mutes in play, and with all bass drum
    mallets and snare drum sticks absent,
the cymbal players faced outward their brass
    shields, taking care that never two
metal plates should cah-lash and destroy the
    oath of council. This parade was
to reflect a new origin altogether.

Oh wow! A perfectly waxed squad car, lights
    blinking toward convulsion status
with reds and blue hues circling like teacup
    joy rides at a carnival: joyous
silence made to order as the officer inside blankly
    smiles at the street-lined assembly.

What a collective, indeed, a grouping of fire engines,
    surrounded by young cheerleaders in full mime
    prosecuting their case for attention with jumps and
    leaps and pom-pom finesse. But no thanks, the
    crowd seems to be saying. We won't give you an A
    or any other letter—not today, not at this parade.

Yes, there he is, a man without whom we locals
    would surely vaporize into void,
our town mayor, Mr. Tinkles, and without a
    voice to infringe upon our sensibilities,
anyone with a heart and tax-exempt status might
    exclaim: "He really does try! Heck,
he's not that bad of a mayor at all, absent his voice,
    which seems to begin his troubles."

The day is turning out quite lovely indeed.

Our silent parade took on in due course a
    meditative quality in which its owners
and participants alike began to fall deeply
    into a state of transcendence.

All clowning stopped at Fifth Street. The
    clowns each in turn wiped from their
faces their respective persona, setting aside
    their props—red sponge noses, plastic
trick flowers, as well as their redundant
    rainbow-permed wigs.

The tallest figure, Mr. Hopkins, who by day
    operated a local grocery store,
collapsed alongside his clown clothing and
    began to fracture the structured silence

of the day by crying out a rhythmic jolt of
　　sobbing composition, at odds entirely with
　　his character. When the five-year-old son of
　　the mayor jetted about to console him,
the entire crowd in sync fell to its collective
　　knee and joined hands in hopes
of winning back the silence from Mr. Hopkins
　　and his overtaken status as the
overly emotive being.

I kept my eyes on the rain clouds that were at
　　once in full attendance. The cymbal players set
　　down their shields; the sun had now forcibly
　　been removed. The day was in question.

No one could bring himself to leave, even as a slow
　　dripping of unmeasured rain started up forces and
　　pulled rank on sun and cooled the back alleys and
　　blocked streets alike. It was as if God's photographer
　　had placed a spell upon our people. And now
　　locked into a still, not even the last dairy farmer in
　　the county, Mr. Chumbs, was free to say cheese!

Frozen, stuck, left nudely ever-present, I imagined
　　myself reaching out to Mr. Hopkins. I would rest
　　at his side, gently fold his hand over mine.

"Mr. H., I understand, I really do. The world is
　　the clown, isn't it Mr. H.? And it's as
if we are the makeup covering over whomever
　　it needs to become. And at times,
it doesn't know who it is or who it ought to be. It's left absent
　　inside, a clown within a clown unsure of itself, except
　　that when it checks, it still pulls a pulse, holds a beat,

even when it has lost its mallets, muted its trumpets, or silenced its figurative existence altogether."

I am here at the center of our town telling you of this tale. From all four sides, the car horns are layered, delivering a conversion from their drivers, screaming that I remove myself at once. But I will stand here in silence, marking time until our council meets again, until a proper vote holds that all parades ought to happen in silence—if for no other reason other than it gives us, the people, a change.

A Didion Moment

You may just find it's no longer a linear landscape
that measures the spaces
in between water and muscle or
that ragtime piano piece
your grandmother marked as her favorite.

Tempo and surprise win over the pragmatic.

Stay with me; I'm about to make the case.

Some days call for us to set down our dreams
and ideals in order to take up with a specific
rationale—certain laws of mathematics,
or a time-honored logic used to keep the patriarchal
money machine finely tuned and relevant.

Our history holds it, almost like an oath we
sputter from our mouths at two months into
this American fervor of glorious pain and blue.

The professor keeps up his end with literature
and an offering to remind the student,
twenty years removed from his classroom,
stories and poems will always be an option,
to push out the clamor brought about
by a tired and overwhelmed wife and
two underwhelmed teenagers.
Read them, recall days of cigarettes
    and coffee house freedom,
or the first after-party in which you

felt honored and were introduced to Guinness
or a Spanish wine, which felt all at once overly
foreign and new to you, or those campus girls
in spring splayed upon the hills as you walked
by spying the good stuff: possibility without obligation,
the last sweet spot of youth waiting there on the green.

The beleaguered waitress holds up too, barely.
Now, well into her fiftieth year, the coffee
smells like ancient oil pumps left out for too many years,
weathered and nearly in ruins. Yet, still there is
movement and a hurtful squeaking that leaves
the locals wondering as they pass by
if the entire rig shouldn't
be shut down altogether.
Thank you for the tip.

So much splits in a life, doesn't it?

Our very essence, umbilical cord snipped, a divide.
Our first love becomes untethered
and more heartbreak presents before
we soldier through minors and majors,
soft-stepping through minefields,
only to be blown up and reintroduced
into life's cannon. Fire!

In our mid-twenties
we find (unceremoniously)
change torments our heart.
The music, your girl, your job
serve now only to displace
your pleasures
or simply to announce:
You can't stay here any longer.

You wake up, naked as a tea cup, hopeful
as a field of wild blueberries,
strong as Beowulf before the dragon.
You decide to be a part of the Big People.

You reengineer your feelings
about life, commitment. A persona
in the making rises up and all but
removes the mechanics of your old nature.
The days forward divide men from
those aging boys in their thirties
who still frequent the downtown dive bars,
living and drinking in a world
of listless memory: their inability
to grow is their only prized possession.
Fill 'er up!

But a man must confute his time
in the linear; and a woman will
assist.

Genesis be damned!

There need be no need to retreat from
within your truest self. Your persona
and its endless varieties exist only
as a utilitarian demand.

You can't co-opt a correct heart.
You shouldn't follow a path not your own.
You can't read another man's words
and keep as your own the very context
clues he's offered only for himself.

Now, my grandmother has passed.

But the song that's playing is fresh and new
each morning of each new season.
It's not Joplin or Turpin or Mozart
by mistake.

It's a man's will in play and always
at stake.

Counting Rivulets

Oh, my friend, the rain has decidedly
declined; the sun shall not then arrive
anytime here soon by reservation alone.

So late into the hours of man I can
but sit still as drying paint upon canvas
can be viewed from any number of dimensions.

Your cool lens of skin settles in
between our bookend hearts
still in revolution over
turning desires undecided
the purest of propaganda you
get me. In other words,
I have you finally.

The rain has dropped in again
to say, speckled rivulets
tippled top puh-tap
slid away down the siding
in and around our minds.

Kiss me now or be done with us
altogether.
Dismiss the now or forever
deliver the unknown sequence
of chance. Go ahead—they're just lips.

White Blood over Red Doves

Gone to the millipede red drops of white cells
counting down contiguous reliance
upon nanonerves and
surf shop ocean blues remembered.

Remember?

Now, you see that ligament longing?

Love for some of us, a tragic
heart-crash,
a scene set alongside a wild lemon wedge
and a wrongly painted used shotgun,
the one your father left behind (for the deed).

Half-mile starvations of albino crows
memorizing their enemy—this illness within.
Red tag beggar's court of unfinished souls
speaking out of body and context with all
content removed; here we have no brevity.

I love X is never going to get done what
needs doing after the impulse of X subsides.
A riddle or rudiment tied into a "know" looks
like a hairy, crazed, toothless prisoner smiling.

Aim for his dentures, dammit!

Okay, do you see that, that's the unspoken word. Speak
   it one more time and this poem blows. Right?

Really, really? You think poetry is a good idea?

I do. You know I said before (it) I do.
Think poetry over you is the only way to go.

Now, thank you, I will. I do. Thank you.

An Extinction Denied

Think a painted Crustaviory
abandoned before the
lungs of that second son
stretched with no response

or

age: this allotment
of life counting out loud
our insular molecular
draw-down. Next,

the voices exclaim,

be gone by way of the eighth poet
in a circle of tenors, ranges locked,
Hume at the helm singing desires,
beating out Descartes and all
that seeks to reason

our existence

exposed,
a tributary of fear runs full measure
through the black cotton fields of the 1840s
or a time that sealed too many fates:
the buffalo, the American Indian,
those drops of race that now resist a full
absorption into our history.

It's all become mercury: inert. Here

think a sculptured iris of Endymion
caught fish-eyed dead, staring through
lifetimes of sleep; he, removed from those
lost centuries of man's pestilence and
    grandeur; he, waiting like an icicle

to melt and drip new life upon
some deaf skin of this existence,

oxygen running through the
son's lungs, holding onto to the eighth poet,
sacrificing his own rage as

the chalcogen brothers divide semitones before
the lamp fires of their forgotten harmonies,
rolling vapors over man's last orb.

All that extinction sings
for me this day owns
us, like Cicero's letters:
seeds for the Enlightenment
sprouting thought-figs and
idea-rich movements that
split Newton's apple and gave
us a renewed wonderment among the living.

It has brought me here,
weary from causality,
too many years without so much as a
dove touch of love or epicurean type exchange.
The blue from my eyes nearly stolen away,
left in time

over time we foot the trails of our pains
and accept barren rewards only to
arrive on some sun-strewn day,
turning our eye toward the great cumulonimbus cloud,
where its unforgiving vortex studies our
ineptitude at being human.
Here a cold rehearsal for the absolute extinction
governed over by my imagined
god Crustaviory:

Sit, listen, and for once cradle this delicate
    freedom in your hand
as you would have a child cling so effortlessly to his smile.

Your Move

The burdens are many as wolves howl is the
    night's stars pronounced in the heavy.
The burdens are unending as crows spy is the
    sun's eye unannounced in the bevy.
To allow to that degree one's feelings,
certain genes turned on.

To allow to that degree one's aching,
transient emotions turned over and over
again.

Your internal metronome is made solvent;
    agreements are now in play. Tick, tock.

Consider what might have gone differently …
the baseball game, age twelve; the game
    of spin-the-bottle, age ten;
or the cock-certain corporate entrée into earning
    a living that surprised even a cynic,
to what we will do to one another for money.

You don't hear that?

London's wolves are thinning, and the
    ancient hurt is no longer deferred.
Agreements are now in play, I tell you.

Look at you in this room full of ghosts.
The only door going out is on constant
lockdown, while your soul keeps winging it

like a flock of falsified memories,
truth, a stem-cell-project in the distance.
You no longer have rights here.
Look at you in this room filled with history.
The only freedom is a maturity
unrequited.

There are, after all, agreements in play.
So, what's your move going to be?

An Owl's Dream

That steadfast black cat
to procure
X
under a sparkled azure sky-life

staring head-beam moment
in
two bee-bee golden wise eyes.

An
owl hoots twice, sings low
cello, bass clef
left flirting with counter
rhythmic syncopation:
ah oooh, ah oooh!

You barely lip-kiss
your nearly empty
teacup, leaving
only vanity to
your imagined
spell-of-a-life.

ah oooh, you who?

Necessary Days

These will convert years from now as
    strange yet necessary days.
The pointed pitch of one hundred yellow warblers
ably seated in concert about your young
    oak tree's scrawny limbs.
About the failing health of the older neighbor lady,
who once outpaced all in the summer lawn competitions,
we know very little these days.
An old boss remembered: "And all like this ..." he would say,
with his southern six-foot-three frame couched horizontally,
toes tip-kissing the back of a gold-plated offering:
Vice President, Information Services.
Then his sigh, just before the lunch hour and as
the meeting is about to adjourn, "Clifford,
    my boy, Ohio is a piss-poor affair
for a white-collar man whose roots run too
    deep into the Kentucky bluegrass."

Somehow you shrink with amazement in your understanding
that their dimorphic plumages are the
    critical bits of information
necessary, like days, to identify their lores
    and cross reference your own
look and feel. (What do you do, placed
    outside of a single point of view?)
The warbler flits by design, migrates out
    of his perpetual instinct.
The oak tree rises into the blue hollow of our American skies.
The VP lives only long enough to retire
    and die shortly thereafter.

To self, then. Think of all that is possible,
    as if has been auctioned
off to your favor. You own what is left,
    not assuming any net result.
You take up where once a promising joy
endeared you, a woman, a career, the
    faith of a couple of bucks
to give willfully to the waitress, who's had less of a career
and more of a displaced purpose serving
    smiles and suggestions
that convert simply as scrambled eggs and ham.

To self, okay. Work from here in the affirmative.
Whistle, you little warbler; grow, you promising oak,
and forget about the crestfallen dreams of dead people.

Win this one, dammit. Win it and convert
    the as if into necessary days.

Aging Shade

After all of your hurt spills over,
try, son, to allow
that a human at its root cause
is an undiscoverable system.

Your studies here are among
the maps of circuitry,
anatomy or illness played
out in perpetuity.

The meaningful remnants of our
hearts are preserved only
in the aging shade.

There, we are amazed and awestruck
how first love cured our temperament
and confusion between being young
and turning old;
how real and independent achievement
makes us feel whole and worthwhile;
or how it arrives full bodied and soulful.
We lose that light center of personhood
after the death of our grandmother,
who still sings to us in a local
park as a peach sky orb dies out
after surveying its own existence,
accepting calm as its antidote,
drawn in fully by a comfort and closure
in perpetuity.
This is the aging shade that must
come over all of us
in perpetuity and otherwise.

Nothing to Be Done

As the final leaf in the civilized world
    breaks from its natural tether,
its universal ghosts will awaken from
    across the multitiered planets
to design the unimaginable under the
    constraints of nothing here foretold.

You will watch the lone spheres.
Exonerate certain paths and arteries,
into which man's locked condition
holds on to itself like a misguided missile.

You will trace the planetary dots into form.
You will erase the honorary flaws that store.

The calcium and vitamins and a soil unrehearsed
will with life rise as an undiscovered
insect, embedded into the core alert system.
The filaments will compound
by the minute into a stronghold of fibrous life stock.
The roots will be wed
and produce without limit a living gangrenous
tissue
followed inbound with reversible muscle and mass.

I will wait for a sign
to do my part; but by then,
there is nothing to be done—
nothing, I tell you.

Once Off the Trail

Dos Equis iced,
tapped, drafted like an unassuming
citizen
only into this frozen mug my day
is here
after the birds have winged it
long tail down south or up
into Canada.

This, a spirit of isolation.
More abandonment looking
out over cast white sheets placed
over a heavenly gray fortress of nil.

Why should it be so?
Opportunity in the offing,
new trails down which my feet alone
will step and counterstep the next
days, months, and years, put upon
my being with a strange newness.

Still, like a deer on the running trail:
one of us here is the foreigner.
Each now
locked in its respective cavity,
musculoskeletal limbs frozen.
We stare deep into the other's eyes.
This one deer spies my being,
removes my heart only to offer it
back, gentle and renewed, nothing
here now disparate or uncertain.

We are not the dominant sun or moon,
not among nature's singing creatures.
We are not above the nuclear
response or the hate-of-heart that
keeps us circling those proverbial
lost American and global-strapped wagons.

Our hearts are small bursts of goodness
ensnared necessarily by a dark human
ego of hundreds of thousands of years
of rehearsal; the same game or plan
unrevised, just a dull vision connected
to a cumulative detached American retina.

But today, let us see through this deer
a cautionary tale nested within
this wooded womb,
drawn back and off the trail.
Be still; isolation is unavoidable.
But so, too, is recovery.

Did you hear that?

Brotherly Worlds

Oh brother, what worlds of worry
would you say
have divided from their parent moons
to deliver such distance at our feet,
such gray malaise in your lifeless eyes?

Our boyhood laughter, all but forgotten,
syllabic echoes endlessly
spiraling through
millions of years that constitute mesmeric
mazes intertwined with thoroughbred
stars racing our memories
away, into some brilliant accretion
disc of infalling material—a supermassive
black hole of familial refuse.

Our tale for a minute in the hour that has
become our lives was a glimpse,
was normal and filled with a healthy
glow of what life may have otherwise
brought us were it not down to this.

Mother, father, two sons aligned, in heart
a ritual churning out goodness and curiosity,
consumed with newness of all variety.
Young Christian family in a portrait
pursuing the predisposed bought and sold
American household: 628 Woodland Drive.
But God didn't bless us enough, did he?

Can you say on the whole of it when
you began to resent my very existence
in this world of earthly defeats?
A birthday party, a boyhood fight ... I know,
I do know, it was none of that. The keystone
that was our father once
removed, structures changed,
and no pieces thereafter would hold up.
Is this what recalibrated your sense of me?
No longer a brother as such.
It was then, I can see now, you left your
brother, as if cutting off a cancerous
piece of skirt steak, pitched now into
the hole.

Feeding it to the pain-tamed
monsters of our beloved and guilty cosmos.

Did you win? Did you survive?
Is hurt the prize you surmised it to be?
Is fear more able than man?
How does this human machine really work?

You and others say I should go,
go and see the old man.
He's now little more than a poorly
drawn parody, loss of height,
atrophic muscles slimmed down to
his shrinking bones, his shirts
draped too long, like an October scarecrow
pushed out as some seasonal aesthetic.
To someone, he's just the old neighbor guy
that routinely forgets to collect his
his garbage can from the curb.

Go, it'll do you
some good. Good.

But you no more hold influence
over me.
Time and intention have seen to it.
I lost a lot back there, brother.
Along with the waste went goodness
as well, and in great measure, I would
say.

Our bond has all but been defeated,
cutting each of us from our genetic tether
of love and family, innocence, for god's sake,
out here in a world of perpetual loneliness.

One wonders if the gun he stored in their
back closet might have taken care
for all of us, to remove what suffering
has held us like an abandoned and crippled
heart, whose valves and veins,
our very arteries, have not worked,
the blockage, a backwards flow for which
I am unable to mitigate its annual damage.

You hope friendship or a career or reading
that one book might restore its ambition
as a necessary part of your human machine.
You get down to the ground floor some nights,
so disassembled your life appears only
as thousands of puzzle pieces, all the same
shapes and colors, with no discernable
construct, nothing any human should
be prepared to reengineer.

Oh brother, what worlds of worry
would you say
have divided from their parent moons
to deliver such distance at our feet,
such gray malaise in your lifeless eyes.

I see you turning in the October clouds,
like a mid-level casino man,
playing the house odds up against
happiness, certitude, a perfectly
stacked grouping of unicorns
blocking an artery,
defining a
sovereign loss
indefinitely.

No One

No one is to blame.
No one is to hate.
No one is to hurt.
No one is to this as yes two are forgiven.

No one is to suffer.
No one is to endure.
No one is to forgive.
No one is to that as this is to be enlightened.

In the end there is no end to begin,
is the science of accelerated gravity
and nothing more
but calculations out of boredom
and human events too dull for discourse.

The center is out like Copernicus.
Out like an overzealous gay rights
marathon runner taking one for the team.
"Go get 'em, Howard!"

No one is curious.
No one is courteous.
No one is cognizant.
No one is above or below the no one is here.

In like pop culture rule of law:
political dereliction.
In like absence, as in reasoning
applied.

In like feelings without cerebral context.
In like a country that's taken its lobotomy
and is headed in due course for utter ruin.

A real scorched earth,
Napoleon, Lord Kitchener,
Sherman, or Stalin.

No one is left behind.
No one will have a sign.
No one will deny

the heart will be obliterated
its
valves left like bloody rubber,
dolls with their heads
sliced off like Sunday ham surprise,
waiting in some Muslim sun
country: prayer is off the table
yet somehow is always being served.

No one is left.
No one was right.

October Embers

The next fall within the October embers fires in
    our minds truths about getting colder.
Your youth and unpredictable summers splayed
    out by all that your memories reveal.

Here alone
consider what has gone absent: curiosity, the
    lightning nectar of love's forbidden root.
Here alone
decipher what algorithms of the heart are still
    stalled by benign neglect or overuse.

It can still in the ripest hour bring this grown man back,
the way your name parsed out from her being
    as she waved from her goodbyes,
the highway hellos and endings when all was promise
and easily negotiated and gotten. It was not all
    deserved, but it arrived nonetheless.

It was all thrift-store goodness, layered
    in a sovereignty of bodies,
coupled in youth's upswing and dalliance.
If worry was a part of it, neither showed it
    or on the whole felt it as such.

There with you
my form took shape,
decided unanimously where it could
    go—skybound, to be sure,

rearview mirrors of multiples, those punch-peach sunslopes
   held up by some unknown force. There with you I
   crawled into adulthood and foretold the making and
   measure of your body, opened up into its youth before
   the governed years turned our idyllic desires to granite.

Our last kiss must have damned us altogether.
Your reliable marriage, my obsession with isolation.
And to think of it now
recalls the next fall, how it is again upon us.
I want as a child wants, to have again the
   security and blind awareness
of touch, how you always held on a little tighter than needed.
You must have known.

The next fall within the October embers fires in
   our minds truths about getting colder.
I am there, my love, loss a part of it, pain too, but mostly
a chill that suspends my free will to
ever feel that way again.

Perilous Pendulum

Your summer,
broken legs crawling home.
Those closed doors are
locked with you
outside.
Your pride, bare-breasted
black bush devil,
spoken tongues.

You sing in the key of puh!

So wilted, too far away, your childhood
sunbeams set on Taser.
Lisa, the kiss, the BB gun fights,
or old man Arthur set up
on his porch like a mannequin in
an amusement park pop gun gallery.

If you are still real, alive to the outward-facing world,
answer me this one question:
How would you know?

If you are still in this,
say as much, utter promise, squeeze
our hand, let up from all that has
been brought to bear:
pressures of day, frustrations,
unstoppable mazes; solve,
administer, free yourself.
You hold sovereignty in your soul,
express its genes, deliver its goods,
and stop this perilous pendulum:
sans dink, dink, dink.

Killing A Matador

Year upon groaning year we are steered further
	from all that once encouraged
our waking hours to be filled with curiosity.

We desire in our exits: school, the job,
the exhausted lovers, to leave these city
limits, be herded elsewhere, into the countryside
or into a ring to assemble our parts
of dying and crossing that proverbial bar.

Year after aching year we take on
circumstances that serve in the end
to leave loneliness where once a
kind word or touch was rehearsed repeatedly.

God, how long has it been for you?

Forget the comforts, the paid bills, or the
top dog that will always be well fed.

Consider the teenager who is innately at
	odds with the parent, the teacher,
or oftentimes himself … because he sees
it all with the intensity of a matador.

The years running at us with a muscled
and nearly unbeatable bulk
with the expressed intent of punctuating a
	certain agitation-turned-rage forward
into a plain conversion of pain and defeat.

The young are remembering future tense
in the present stance of their being:

Six bulls to the metaphor
turn, multiples
a square root goes cubed,
and the math of human fear is upon us.

Age, day one to puberty is our singing the
    benediction before the barrier is removed.
Saint Fermin et al., we love these traditions.

A running of the bulls personified
blowing out our inside walls of mind
and manners and lessons wasted
on the corrupt adult world,
deferring this reality with shows and lies,
decrying a polluted this or that when
the only pollutant is the asshole who
wakes and gets trained like a dog to mind
his cubicle and not wander beyond
his leash length, while race baiters go
fishing for bullshit, hull it up by the pounds
and piss on tradition and sensibility.

It doesn't take a child over the age of
ten to tap into the adult psyche,
and it won't seem wrong to them when the
matador gets what's coming for him
wholesale, a
certain agitation-turned-rage racing forward
into a plain conversion of pain and defeat

wholesale, tax included!

Happy Demons Dance

My cold demons with their arthritic limbs ably
hurting through arctic storms

upon frozen lip-tripped kiss-can'ts
and the blankest of conversations. Why
ain't love a little more than super cruel?

You wired me, encrypted the code in stereo.
I desired you, determined that a future fought
without you as monastery was no church at all.

Now, we say about all of this nothing.
End time.

Be loved and be grateful, yet still, never
after you or me or that which arose
out of the cosmos: satisfied. Don't ask
that of me, not while I am still among the dead.

Now, I command you, happy demons dance!

Waking in California

It is a raw almond honesty
revised and
slipped through with piano fingers
and black lace
twirling a curl then flat to the ivories:
C major chord records the evergreen
notes. We don't play them anymore.

She kissed me as much as time and
space between us; the whole note rests,
the dynamics in accord with her rhythms.

Oregon junco
and friends scratch and whistle only
feet on the other side of her perfectly
framed woman design
flesh
fruit
hope
veins running and routing her pain
through happiness over calcium

warm skin wondering if and how
goodness can ever be contained
heart
mate
faith
cells turning off and on our lives
a limbic system reserve for it all.

Yes, I do remember waking in California.
Here now oddly removed years
gutted, a pumpkin carved out and
tossed away post-holiday for cars to thrash
its orange flesh, until there are but a few
chunks resting curbside like ones
feeling after the kissing draws down
and you don't say much to each other.

Give it time, patience; it'll reach you.
Things don't usually work out for the best,
and the least of it you are holding onto
right now—a memory held up posthumously

and you are no longer a part of it.

Whitman's Early Birds

Upon first chirp the overlays begin
amidst a sky morning chorus
soaring
wings that connect imaginary lines,
soon a pure whistling
rings throughout,
as if in some alternative continuum
Whitman is here,
himself recast as a singing chorus
of morning birds. Blessed are we;
this poem is a concert for our soul.
You assume your very bones and
their lapped upon muscle and circuitry
in a way never before imagined.
The birds cast out and recast
coda and coda again, slinging earthly
chirp into universal song. Blessed
are those who hear in their pitch
the slant notes: never perfect, only wonderful
still, all the same
still.
Human once mimicked their nature,
this highbrow orchestra:
first chair chickadee, second
chair piccolo, the yellow warbler.
No, not scales exactly; this is more
fantastic,
as in a language when all grammar
gets applied not evenly or commensurate
to its rules; rather, when it says

the ordinary in remarkable fashion,
grounded, never aloof, simple, and always
steady to its target: the human
heart arrives open
like a bird's soul, wide as genius,
solid as oak, and ready beyond all
to live!

Blue Squirrels

our fear is we may have lost him
inside of himself. i can assure you,
variations are in play:

multi-layered semi-muted revolutions
of static, actualizing unwanted versions
of self, himself decrying it all against wobbling
interiors of uneven screams
sent forth: iambic based
genetic expressions of rage.

is balance no longer an option? (i'm asking you)

he is becoming his own uncontrollable fugue
only the tones, their fundamental makeup and purpose
risk a permanent displacement along his universal linear—
here the logic has gone rogue, its more subtle links
deteriorated, unable to keep up, the threads
and assembly mix to create new
unreliable pidgins within his upper and lower
emotional genus; but no, nothing is calling on proper
communication, the whole exercise is an
        unusable circular system of defense.

is reason no longer an option? (now i'm telling you)

he continues the requests for blue squirrels.

blue squirrels. squirrels in a world of blue.
their tails, he insists, contain cosmoline.

their efforts mirage the inventory, keeping
a specialized weaponry
preserved and hidden. he continues the requests,
    I repeat, he continues his requests
for blue squirrels—blue squirrels in a
    world of blue squirrels again

and again with the blue squirrels.

our fear is we've lost you, that you
have further drifted

so i'll ask you once more,
have we lost you somewhere in that
    dissolving dray of blue squirrels?

The Firefly Metaphor Poem

It may be the last tulip she spies,
leaving the office Friday at five.

It could be a faulty bra strap
she curses Wednesday morning,
late for yet another meeting.

More than likely, however, it's going to be a
    memory that was semantically written to
her hippocampus during those periwinkle
    years when our minds and bodies
are left fully open and free.

It will be after the kids are well into their
    dreamland, the husband, too, neatly
affixed and emotionally foreclosed on his La-Z-
    Boy, looking more like a chalk
outline at the scene of a crime
than a well-intentioned grown man,
a time when the fireflies begin their majestic flight.

The bitty yellow tail blush
spine-checks her entire life
within the millisecond. Her own cells
fill in deeply to recall the kind of continuous kiss
we most always leave behind save for what
    memory's pleasure affords us
during chilling bouts of loneliness,
left in some uneasy chair of life's default.

Her attention is caught as they create their light enzyme
and compete in this natural world of order.
The female fireflies sideline to judge those
    J-shaped dips designed to exclaim what
we humans do without subtlety or shame: "Hey,
    look at me! Look, over here; I'm worthy ..."

But as the night pours too much into her, she'll reach
to dismiss the needle from her old childhood record player.
Chopin's Nocturne No. 7 in C-sharp minor cut short again.

She doesn't discount the marriage or regret the kids.
She doesn't remove her foreground feelings
for the sake of an emotive backdrop in her past.
She doesn't assume life may ever change.

She just closes the blinds and divorces
herself from the sight of those fireflies
and all they must imply—
her own dying cells,
the continuous kiss
that keeps us all starving
within our own natural world.

Period

Today I'm held up by endless inches
of the white sun stare glowing east
from off of my neighbor's rooftop—
sterile, winter aging thusly; and yet
all is luxury, isn't it?

Depression. My father's absence,
his abuse of alcohol, my mother,
or his unwillingness to be an honest man.

The world has no shortage of real
tried and true heartache. Real
humans suffering so badly and deeply.
There is no time for those people
to consider personal sadness on some
reflective level of personal intuitiveness.
They don't say things like, Oh, gee,
I didn't realize the time, but I've got a
4 o'clock with my therapist. No,
this is all luxury; and you hope humility
makes you aware of the fact.

The bourbon, the warm home setup
in a suburban Midwest town. Those
ex-girlfriends you once-and-again consider
calling, if time were not the variable that it is,
or the way in which you earn a living: is it a
        job, a career, a title, or position that is
necessarily what enables others' perception
of us? Luxury.

There are young girls on other continents
not thinking or obsessing over when they'll
start their period. They are, rather, scared to death over
    when the next foreign businessman will enter their room
    and rape them, systematically remove all hope and
    heart from their very essence of personhood. Period.

Meanwhile,

I can't locate that damn can of chicken noodle
    soup I bought last week. I've checked every
    cupboard twice. It must be here, shouldn't it?

I need to get in the car and drive to the
    store and buy another can.

Gas. Stores. Cars. Money. Time. Luxury.

You hope humility makes you aware of the fact,
    and sometimes, twice on Sundays.

Period.

Chapter Statics1
There is for me in this, horrific nights spent in damaged
memories, left as revolving emotive dissident molecules.
I dare not touch,
their sense descends

---

[1] Statics is the branch of mechanics that is concerned with the analysis of loads (force and torque, or "moment") on physical systems in static equilibrium, that is, in a state where the relative positions of subsystems do not vary over time, or where components and structures are at a constant velocity. When in static equilibrium, the system is either at rest, or its center of mass moves at constant velocity.

into caught locked eggshells filled each (one by one)
with baby black caimans, waiting like the insides
of native ideas, of some acknowledged voltage or kicked-off
uncontained joules raging energy through the
dampened spine of a blue-eyed boy holding all breath out
as if to say: I, too, refuse to be born to you.

Its river runs raw, and its micro birds tweet routinely
at exactly 100 kHz. The bottom roots call in turn
to determine what here is life and what here must go away.

And when the snow begins its fall from the bottom upward
into the moon layers, I can't stop thinking of her or
her endless prehensile processes,
wading and collecting me with her velvet tentacles,
each assuming my audition for her heart.

But still, it's the remainder of that mental tentage,
arranged encampments, the cactus summers untamed
that hold out
breath for water, air for life,
a fligtamoyepheral space: my relative position of subsystem
does not vary over time any longer, will not commit to your
statics …

Denied

We know in this human condition the heart
has the capacity to fill and still manage
our deepest pains, our unfulfilled expectations,
    and maybe—just maybe—
still reach out and attempt a new kiss,
so fragile
to touch, this mechanism distilling
days of discomfort, looking always to
trade in years of unrest for a bold,
yellow, hopeful sunrise—tomorrow, if possible.

The test, we now know, is without
boundary or delay, the pressing
always in play.

The day, and then it never happened again,
her face and eyes and overall warm cache
convinced me: love is but a second falling
through millions and possibly trillions
of causal anomalies throughout our lives
until as with static or white noise personified
it, the second, goes missing

with all that missing implies
when once the hardest truth about us
was in play

children, joy, evolution of a young boy

denied.

The Ice Fish Poem

Lately those dreams I kept just don't sync.

And look at me. This aging face is erasable,
    just melted snow from a streetscape
dead long ago, spring new,
a snapshot of joy removed
and hours, only hours, out of a man's life
in which pain did exactly as it was told.

There is a risk to this, I admit, reaching into such icy waters
to lose all warmth, expel the intrusions,
to find a new life underground.

Turned ice fish, losing hemoglobin, no need any longer
for oxygen as such; a test in evolution:
adapt and lose all that others
insist is necessary.

Wait translucent. You see right through your brain and gills
to receive in new ways your essence,
here to insufflate its air, rising and falling out
absent, the peril of any human imposition.

Oh my, how glorious is this?

A fish
free heart at last.
No hooks,
no nets or traps,
only cello waves of white,

a kind of aloneness set to repeat
in sync with new systems. Only
this time my dreams align,
the calibration complete. Begin!

Sweet Discovery

Here we sit,
circled and barely connected. I had hoped by now
you might say anything, just one thing
that assumes or implicates me as a part of this family.
(No, you stare inside of static-charge silence,
approach me as the hatred of your condition.)

There you wait,
engulfed and rarely rejected. You had hoped by now
I might take everything or just the death punches
that might serve to annihilate me from being a part of this.
(Yes, I stare into your charged silence, seeing
        you as the hatred of this rendition.)

My only ally no longer speaks, her body set
        into soil, her soul turning musical
notes into root melodies that no longer hear the
        subspecialty of their indefinite tones.
This far into loneliness, a man hunts for his
        survival, turning over language
like soil, but without a proper squat pen or
        father, he feels the full breadth
of his skin thinning, caught like shoestring leather
        in these blank gears called our life machine.

His drinking becomes the enchanted forest to the north;
        the south calls upon him to die at will. The corpse
        cannot settle, and the house never had a home

this far into loneliness this far into the brutal years. Here the
    ocean draws from rage down to slurps, where human
    kindness arrives like a thirsty animal—the edge,
reach, slurp in the now-distant feelings of
    what once it felt like to be human.

Gasp like a dying worker bee: mate then die;
    surprised to wake forward in the next
hive you spot the lost honey of your days, a sweet discovery.

Nothing Happening Beautifully

What haunts and traces us with the exactitude of a fine artist
looms still longingly off the shore's echo
from ocean to moon and through all erasure back to this.

Twin blue eyes through the decade mirrors
pulled in by memory, walking tall inside love's highest
ambition,
turning body under sun to review old feelings anew.

A world whispered; did we hear?
Lost from her lips, the arc-cadence
of a deaf, dumb drummer without sticks,
swinging through polyrhythmic measures,
and like the emperor who wears no clothes,
he, too, marches aloof, alone, a mere pebble dropped
through the universe, consigned to oblivion.

But here their stamp on history, her twin brown eyes
spying endless fields of daffodils
performing orchestral trills
fluttering beneath a million monarch butterflies,
swarming after the deep breath of a secrecy lost,
a mental montage of how we wish life to sit still,
like a first sketch or idea realized: Stop!

I won't ask this of her or anyone, to recall any part
of me, my unbalanced footsteps over life,
the well-documented delusions of normal personhood.

But what I will do, what I will assume

is nothing happening beautifully
like a heart rendering itself useful in the midst
of a first kiss resolved.

Tire with him no more. The decade mirrors
sans reflection; and this time, our time, is now disposed of.

Ischemia

The ardent fruit long ago
hung metaphor in a foreground
casting slit shadow lines
over your lover's body
as she waited too long for
seed, for some natural change
to take and shape her anew.

Now these aberrant mappings
crawl tirelessly through a casting
of labyrinth after labyrinth
mind and mischief. Boredom
is their love
falling in and out of phase,
the bellows of internal pain,
notions slow, until two hearts
stop on go, leaving most
everything that mattered
to one last cold kiss,
lips chapped and love
consigned to oblivion.

You ought to know for future
reference what is absolute
when it comes to the impressionable
longing in our open heart
of hearts: oxygen, blood
pushing
full-on through our superior vena cava,
thoughts accompanying it up,

passing the mitral valve.
Oh, aorta, aorta, what have you done for me lately?

Ischemia, dance with me one last time
the dance of constriction;
allow that our eyes settle in a waltz.
Any key you like will do.
We move like ardent fruit
captured and crunched into,
the core of us left in measures
pianissimo. The light favors us,
and you'll have your way,
and I'll be your final
three steps into my forever smile.

Department Store Sighting

for Krista

When I saw you with your daughters in that department store
after nearly two decades of absence, I was
    not prepared for my own sorrow.
The woman I was with was not my wife;
    I have no wife or children.
For the minute that I spied you, you were in perfect form,
pointing at the screen, providing tutelage to the young
ones. And who that knows you would expect anything less?

Your face appeared tired, the real thing that proves a woman
or man has been making the most of their life.
Your eyes are still uniquely pensive,
your mind, I imagine, still unyielding
to the intellectually impoverished.

I too am tired; and besides,

we've passed the point at which we see one another and
embrace—a painful comfort of loving
    discord for the moment.
Your daughters: how old-timey to have to explain
who the hell I am, was, or might have been.
"You mean there was someone before daddy?"
(It's okay, kids, there'll be no need today.)

It hurts to think about the truth I could
    not then share with you.
Instead, I placed the entirety of it at the feet of your mother.

Her unwavering impulse to check in and
    oversee our time together.
Her unapologetic impulse to kick you when you were down.

I guess we both had our personal hurdles—
My father, abandonment, shame always shelling
me like some bad and uninterruptible tenet
of human condition, endurance our only claim.

There was a great deal I left out.
The day we sat at your piano and cried
so hard our pain couldn't find any
footing to guide us; the ending always
in a state of emotional inconsistency.

Why was this happening to us?

My fear after the engagement
became more than I could control.
An alarming knowledge, that I could continue
to love you in earnest—as I had done for five years;
the realization I could provide you and our
future family with all it needed: the goods,
the foundation a man must know he can provide.
I had none of it.

For my part, it was my father.
He branded me like livestock.
(To whom do we belong?)
I thought I could erase the marking.
But when I looked, even at my best,
I was always less than I could become.

Left for you, little more than a

fervid temperament of useless cynicism.
I could not bring myself
to admit such weakness.
I loved you too much
and myself not enough—
a non-starter in the game of life.

Your husband is a kind and productive man.
We met only once with the agreement:
never tell a soul and never speak again.
He has given you all that I could not.

There's no going back. I'm not trying.

Can we agree on this before I go?
Ireland gave us a glimpse of us
removed from your mother's
oversight and my father's memory.

It allowed for a specific freedom lovers need
in order to understand whether or not
their bodies, minds, and souls
are willing to take on the vast chances of marriage.
We were standing inside of Kilkenny Castle,
reading our notes about Strongbow's
daughter, Isabel.
We both agreed our daughter would be
both beautiful and intelligent,
and we would commemorate all of this
by naming her Isabel.

It was our getting the hell out of Dublin
after a ten-year-old boy randomly grabbed his
crotch and gave us the finger as we turned

around and tried to navigate such newness.
We laughed, and your strength in innocence
always compelled me to remember, there
will never be you again in my life.

It was the moment we landed in Pittsburgh,
two weeks later, hundreds of new memories
made and placed within the privacy of our hearts.
I knew it could not last once we returned
to the model your mother had built for us
or the ruin my father had instilled in me.

Hey, it was good to see you today.
I rarely go out these days,
and department stores are the worst.
I know, we did say hello in our own way,
in that absolute flash second when you
looked over and I turned toward my
cashier, to avoid any awkwardness
either way.
I owe you that much.
What's left is history
playing from one movement
to the next. Our beloved Brahms—
we admired together so much
his Symphony No. 4—
the space from allegro giocoso
to allegro energico e passionato,
from major to minor,
the quiet waiting in between,
like seeing you in that department store
after nearly two decades of absence,
still the music plays.

www.ingramcontent.com/pod-product-compliance
Lightning Source LLC
LaVergne TN
LVHW051630080426
835511LV00016B/2274